Around Manc

in the 1970s

Clive Hardy

iN
iNostalgia

MANCHESTER CONCORDE
MANCHESTER

Around Manchester
in the 1970s

(Above). Telephonists at the Central Electricity Board offices, Wilmslow Road, East Didsbury, work the switchboard by the light of hurricane lamps during the power cuts caused by the energy workers' work-to-rule in support of a pay claim. Work-to-rule meant that employees would do no more than the minimum required by the rules of their employer, rather than take the more militant action by going on strike. 8 December 1970.

(Opposite page). *The Manchester Concorde* passes down the Ship Canal in August 1977, on her way to the container terminal. This picture is unusual in that it was taken from the eastbound lane of the M60 on the Barton Viaduct.

Clive Hardy

Designed by Clive Hardy.

iNostalgia is an imprint of Communities in the Cloud Ltd, Progress Centre, Charlton Place, Ardwick, Manchester.

As part of this book, we are delighted to preserve in print some of the wonderful memories we receive every day on our iNostalgia Facebook page. We greatly enjoy reading them and we're sure you will too. If you want to join the conversation, just click on our Facebook page. We'd love to hear from you, www.facebook.com/inostalgiamanchester/

Having been relegated to the Third Division at the end of the 1970-71 season, Bolton began a fightback. By the time they were facing York City at Burden Park on 21 April 1973, the whiff of promotion was in the air. Two points would secure promotion. A goal from Pete Nicholson and two more from Stuart Lee did the trick and the fans went wild. The Third Division title was secured with a 2-2 draw away to Port Vale and a 2-0 home win against Brentford on 23 and 28 April respectively. Bolton finished four points clear of runners-up Notts County, and six points clear of third placed Blackburn Rovers.

Introduction

Welcome to *Around Manchester in the 1970s*. Those of you who have had a look at *Around Manchester in the 1950s* and *Around Manchester in the 1960s* know what you are in for. For those of you who are fresh to these books, the plot goes something like this. This book came about following discussions to reprint earlier publications such as *The Changing Face of Manchester in the Seventies* and *Salford Past*. However, one of the points raised was that many of the images had been done to death, having already appeared in other publications and that in all honesty we should include as much fresh material as possible. Also, we decided to expand the number of photographs from around what in 1974 became the Metropolitan County of Greater Manchester, which comprises the boroughs of Bolton, Bury, Oldham, Rochdale, Stockport, Tameside, Trafford, Wigan and the cities of Manchester and Salford.

So here, in a few paragraphs, is a brief description of what life was like in the UK during the Seventies. Many people remember it as a decade of industrial unrest as one strike after another dominated newspaper headlines. Between January and July 1970, more than six million working days were lost due to industrial action. In April 1970, Barbara Castle, Secretary of State for Employment, introduced an Industrial Relations Bill aimed at settling inter-union and unofficial disputes. It was opposed by the TUC and many Labour MPs and the Bill is cited as one of the principal reasons for Labour losing the June 1970 General Election. The incoming Tory administration introduced its own industrial relations policy which in turn led to a prolonged period of industrial unrest. During 1970, there were 3906 strikes (including one by council workers) involving a total of 1,793,000 workers. The following year was slightly better. Although there were only 2228 strikes (including the first ever strike by postal workers), the total number of workers involved was still above one million.

In 1972, the National Union of Mineworkers (NUM) flexed its muscles, calling members out for seven weeks in protest at a £2 a week pay rise offer from the National Coal Board. By mid-February, fourteen power stations had shut due to lack of coal. The problem was compounded when power and railway workers went on an overtime ban and the NUM made effective use of 15,000 flying pickets to impede coal deliveries elsewhere. The Conservative government under Edward Heath declared a state of emergency.

Power cuts were introduced and these normally lasted for three hours at a time, either in the morning, afternoon or evening. The cuts – which were publicised in advance - were rotated so an area would not be affected at the same time every day. Much of British industry went on to a three-day week. Three consecutive days of guaranteed power supply enabled many companies to maintain production, though they were not allowed to put on extra shifts. Interestingly, productivity hardly dropped. The miners returned to work on 28 February and the state of emergency was lifted at the end of the following week. Even so, the NUM strike was just one of 2497 that year.

Monday 15 February 1971 was D-Day. It was the day when the UK would exchange its centuries' old currency of pounds, shillings and pence for decimalisation. The days of twelve pennies to the shilling, twenty shillings to the pound were over. From now on it would be one hundred new pence to the pound. There had already been a gradual move to the new money – the 50p coin had been introduced in October 1969 and the following month saw the withdrawal of the half-crown coin (2s.6d). A year later, the ten-shilling bank note (equivalent to 50p) was also withdrawn and all non-decimal coins were scheduled to be phased out by mid-1973 at the latest. The Decimal Currency Board printed 50million leaflets explaining the new system. Schools and colleges ran decimal money classes for older people and high street stores such as Woolies had 'decimal officers' in every outlet to explain the new money to the bewildered. The *MEN* also ran a series of decimal money teach-ins. Five sessions were organised to take place over 2 and 3 February, but the demand was so great from readers that additional sessions were organised for 4 February at the Lesser Free Trade Hall and the Garrick Theatre, Stockport. Tickets were available from one of the paper's mini vans, which toured different locations at set times of the day. The reason was that although tickets could be got over the counter at the newspaper offices, there was no way of mailing them to readers as there was a strike by postal workers.

Around the Manchester area, SELNEC introduced correct fare decimal buses with conductors onboard to help passengers get into the swing of things. As with the new pound coin design issued in 2017, a fortune was spent converting vending machines and so on to take the new money – the cost to the post office alone to convert telephone boxes was put at £3million.

In 1971, inflation was already running at around 6.4per cent and decimalisation fuelled it even further as prices were rounded up rather than down. There were reported instances of some retailers simply changing old to new – overnight an item costing 2s.4d suddenly became 24p – the difference being that 24p was equal to 4s.8d in old money.

1971 was also the year that Rolls-Royce, having hit development problems with its new RB211 gas turbine engine, ran out of cash. In Derby, where Rolls-Royce was a major employer, rumours ran wild that the company was about to go bust, resulting in a run on the Derbyshire Building Society. Despite appeals from the society that it had sufficient funds, massive queues formed outside its branches as people clamoured to draw out their savings. Rolls-Royce went into receivership and was rescued by the Conservative government which did not hesitate to nationalise it.

General De Gaulle of France had spent years opposing the UK's membership of the European Economic Community but on 1 January 1973 we joined. In 1975, the UK held the first referendum in its history, a simple Yes or No vote to remaining in the EEC. We voted to remain.

In December 1973, in the wake of the Arab-Israeli Yom Kippur War, OPEC announced increased prices for crude oil – effectively doubling the price in just three months. The shortage of petrol was not confined to the UK, it was worldwide. The UK government introduced a 50mph speed limit and considered introducing petrol rationing. The RAF suffered a shortage of aviation fuel forcing it to alter daily operations at UK bases. A friend who was serving with a fighter squadron said it went something like this: 'Wednesday will now be a Tuesday unless it's raining when it will be a Thursday. Fridays are cancelled until further notice'.

The NUM took the initiative by demanding a pay rise of more than double the government's maximum. Power and railway workers again imposed overtime bans. Despite UK trade figures showing a whopping £270million deficit, Prime Minister Edward Heath again imposed a three-day week on the nation. The CEGB issued power supply rotas to the retail trade, though there were no restrictions on retailers opening on other days provided they used alternative sources for heating and lighting. Anyone caught using CEGB supplies when they should not would be liable to a fine of up to £400 or three months in jail. The restrictions threw up a few interesting anomalies. Community centres and old-age pensioners' clubs were not exempt from the restrictions on power but food outlets, strip joints and bingo halls were. TV stations were ordered to close every night at no later than 10.30pm.

By the new year, things were so bad that there was talk of forming a National Government. The pound dropped to what was then its lowest level ever against the US dollar at $2.16 and the governor of the Bank of England became a prophet of doom and gloom, predicting ten years of austerity the like of which we had not seen since the 1940s. On 7 February, Prime Minister Edward Heath called a general election to be held three weeks later under the banner "Who Governs Britain?" On 10 February, the NUM called an all-out strike, though the way it was conducted is interesting in that there was to be no mass picketing – picket lines were restricted to a maximum of six men on each. With the miners still out on strike and the situation getting worse by the day, at least one Tory MP was calling for the setting-up of vigilantes to drive lorries through NUM picket lines. There was now a real prospect of troops being called in. Mick McGahey of the NUM spoke on the radio: "Many of the troops which may be mobilised are the sons of miners, and if they come to dig coal, we shall appeal to them and explain our case to them." On 21 February, the Tories were wrong-footed when the Pay Board published a report on miners' pay that refuted the line put out by the NCB and that the miners were indeed being paid less in comparison with other manufacturing workers.

The General Election finished with Labour on 301 seats, the Conservatives on 297 seats and the Liberals – despite polling six million votes - on fourteen seats. As Labour were short on an overall majority, Heath squatted in 10 Downing Street whilst he attempted to form a coalition with the Liberals under Jeremy Thorpe. When Thorpe rejected Heath's proposals, Harold Wilson formed a minority Labour administration. The NUM called off their strike shortly afterwards. A second general election held in October 1974 gave Wilson a three-seat majority, but by April 1976 it had been wiped out following the defection of backbencher John Stonehouse and MPs Jim Sillars and John Robertson breaking away to form the Scottish Labour Party. Minority and small majority government brought with it the sight of sick MPs being stretchered through the voting lobbies for important divisions. It was said that a doctor was positioned just outside the lobby to examine sick MPs to see if they were still breathing and therefore able to vote.

By the end of 1974, inflation was approaching 20per cent and despite a healthy profit of £51.3million the previous year, British Leyland was in serious trouble. The government had little choice other than to cough up £1.4billion to take a lame duck prone to wildcat strikes into state ownership, though Jack Jones, General Secretary of the Transport and General Workers Union, was all for selling it off to General Motors. Shipbuilding – an industry riven by demarcation disputes - had been

mages from Doreen Spooner's Manchester Fashion Spy' article, *Daily Mirror*, 20 January 1978.

nationalised in July 1974 and the government had also stepped in the save motorcycle manufacturers Norton Villiers Triumph. Though ministers agreed to NVT going bust, the Receiver was told that the 1200 strong workforce would form a co-operative and buy it.

During May 1977, the fuel supply emergency that had started four years earlier was deemed over and UK speed limits were raised to 60mph on single carriageways and 70mph on dual carriageways and motorways.

Even as the decade entered its last year, the country was in the grip of industrial turmoil with 1978-79 being labelled the 'winter of discontent.' Labour Prime Minister, Jim Callaghan imposed a 5per cent pay ceiling with the result that railway workers, bakers, oil tanker drivers, lorry drivers and BBC staff either came out on strike or were very close to doing so. There was also a threat from ambulance crews to ignore 999 calls. What made matters worse for Labour was that Jim Callaghan did an early Theresa May and misread the situation. The only difference was Jim didn't call a general election. Having attended a summit in the West Indies, he arrived back suntanned, relaxed and smiling. The impression it gave was that whilst the rest of us had been battling on, Jim had abandoned his post and gone off on a freebie. The front page of the *Sun* featured a picture of Callaghan with the headline 'CRISIS? WHAT CRISIS.' The result was that Opposition leader Margaret Thatcher called for a vote of no confidence in the Callaghan administration which she won by 311 votes to 310. A general election was called for 3 May 1979 and the Tories swept into power.

In the early 1970s, your average Brit was something of a novice when it came to drinking wine. There were favourites – usually Blue Nun, Mateus Rose or the odd bottle of Frascati or Chianti. French wines had suffered following the publicising of a scam involving cheap Algerian plonk which had been shipped in bulk to Ipswich, where it had been bottled up and passed off under various Beaujolais and Burgundy labels. Serious beer drinkers of taste were deploring the disappearance of the independent breweries. The distinctive flavour of a fine beer served from the cask was becoming an all too rare pleasure, which probably explained why Joseph Holt's Brewery at Cheetham was working at full stretch in response to increased orders for their old-fashioned draught beer. Holt's head brewer, Bernard Angood, told *MEN* journalist Chris Aspin: "There's a reaction against bland keg beers, which are the same from one end of the country to the other." Holt's, which had been based in Cheetham since 1849, had seen sales of its draught beers rise by 11per cent since October 1971.

Even so, it had not forgotten customers who liked keg by investing in a new keg beer plant that would provide extra choice at the company's eighty-four pubs and twenty-two off-licences. At the end of 1971, the company's shares stood at a little under £5 each, and were described as the most undervalued on the market. By August 1972, the share price had risen to £12.25. Oddly enough, Holt's were never subject to a takeover bid though Allied had an 8per cent stake in the business. The campaign for real ale (CAMRA) was founded in 1971 – its aim to revive interest in traditional beers over foreign lagers. I remember friends of mine who were serving with the armed forces in West Germany coming home on leave and looking for pubs serving lager, much of which was bottled rather than being from a keg. The taste for lager and wine was also influenced by the increase in the numbers of Brits taking package holidays abroad. Between 1970-72, the numbers rose from 4.25million to 8.5million, with Spain, North Africa, Austria and Belgium among the favourites, though the more adventurous were getting to Greece and the Middle East.

During the summer of 1976, a belt of high-pressure extending over northern Europe prevented the approach of rain-bearing westerly winds. The situation became desperate. The sugar beet harvest was a disaster, fresh vegetables were in short supply and for a while we were in the grip of the great potato shortage. The cost of that great British staple, a bag of chips, rocketed. Fish and chips was no longer an inexpensive way of feeding the family. Strangely enough, once the shortage was over, the price of chips didn't seem to fall. Plans were drawn up to import water from Scandinavia and, on at least one occasion, some visiting Native Americans were asked to perform their tribal rain dance. The Drought Act was rushed through Parliament, one of its main aims to close loopholes in the 1945 Water Act which could impose hosepipe bans for gardens etc, but not for filling of private swimming pools. The Department of Environment introduced the normal strategy so beloved by British governments of whatever colour – confidential telephone lines encouraging neighbours to grass one another up. Meanwhile, sports minister Denis Howell was made 'minister for drought.' The drought ended in September amid torrential downpours.

During the Second World War, the government imposed price controls on most food prices with the result that there was very little increase in the cost of basic foodstuffs between the early 1930s and the late 1940s. However, between 1949 and 1957, the price of most basic items such as milk, cheese, bread, butter, bacon, flour, eggs, tea and sugar almost doubled.

Inflation during the Seventies makes price comparisons with the Fifties and Sixties interesting reading. In 1957, a 14oz loaf of bread cost 4d. By 1967 it had risen in price to one shilling and by 1977 to 17p (3/5d). Using the same date lines, a pint of milk had gone from 7d to 10d and then to 12p (2/5d); sirloin from 4/2d per lb to 6/10d and then to £1.41 (£1.8s.2d). Streaky bacon had jumped from 2/11d per lb to 3/6d and then to 74p (14/10d). During the same period, the price of a dozen eggs went from 3/10d to 4/1d to 53p (10/7d).

All prices quoted in the introduction and in captions are as they were back in the Seventies. As with the previous books in the series, I have included an inflation calculator so that you can have a bit of fun comparing 1970s prices with those of 2017. For example, an item that cost £1 in 1972 would cost £13 in 2017. So, £1 in 1970 would be £15.10p in 2017, £1 in 1971 would be £14.20, £1 in 1972 would be £13, £1 in 1973 would be £12.10p, £1 in 1974 would be £11.10p, £1 in 1975 would be £9.58p, £1 in 1976 would be £7.71p, £1 in 1977 would be £6.62p, £1 in 1978 would be £5.72p and £1 in 1979 would be £5.28p.

And, for any of you whinging about inflation in 2017, consider the following. In 1970 it was running at 6.4per cent; in 1971 it was 9.4per cent; in 1972 it dropped to 7.1per cent; in 1973 it was up again at 9.2per cent; in 1974 it rocketed to 16per cent; in 1975 it went into orbit at 24.2per cent; in 1976 it dropped to 16.5per cent; in 1977 there was a slight drop to 15.8per cent; in 1978 it almost halved to 8.3per cent and in 1979 it was up again at 13.4per cent.

Furthermore, if you want to moan about income tax, think back to the fifties and sixties when the top rate was set at 90per cent. In 1971, top-rate tax was reduced to 75per cent but a surcharge of 15per cent was applied on investment income which in effect kept the rate at 90per cent. During 1974, the top rate was increased to 83per cent, which with the investment surcharge pushed it to 98per cent – the highest since the 99.25per cent rate set during the Second World War. Top rate was applied to incomes over £20,000 which is around £222,000 in 2017. Margaret Thatcher favoured indirect taxation and the first budget after the 1979 General Election saw the top rate reduced from 83per cent to 60per cent and the basic rate from 33per cent to 30per cent. As well as income tax, back in the 1970s we paid purchase tax on all sorts of items. Between 1940-1973, purchase tax was levied at different rates – at one time the purchase tax on new cars was set at 100per cent, but from 1973 it was standardised at 25per cent. When the UK joined the EEC, purchase tax was replaced by VAT at a standard rate of 10per cent.

The book is divided into sections: *Out and About*, is what it says on the tin – a look around the area from Salford slums to the folly that was Hulme Crescents. We also have the one-and-only Muhammad Ali at the Tesco supermarket, Stretford; there are photographs of shopping centres and retail therapy and the old shambles, perched high up on massive new concrete foundations because of construction work on the Arndale Centre. The section also covers the Silver Jubilee celebrations and Queen Elizabeth II on a walkabout together with much, much, more.

World of Work includes amongst other things photographs of Manchester Liners, Manchester Steel and rescue work following the explosion at Golborne Colliery.

Strikes, Protests and Politics includes dock strikes, the post office strike, protests against closures, the fire brigades strike, general elections and the National Front.

Getting Around? Essentially, but not necessarily, trains, boats, cars, planes.

You're Not Singing Anymore looks at the trials and tribulations of Bolton Wanderers, Manchester City, Manchester United, Oldham Athletic and Rochdale.

Grandstand? includes Lancashire County Cricket Club, Leigh, Salford, Wigan and Warrington Rugby League Football Clubs and Belle Vue speedway.

Rock, Pop, Punk and Northern Soul includes, among others, Wigan Casino, Barclay James Harvest, the Bee Gees, the Hollies, 10cc, Thin Lizzy, the Clash, the Stranglers and the Sex Pistols.

That's Entertainment equals Corrie, cinemas, theatres and Belle Vue Zoo.

This book does not attempt to be an academic work. It is a popular look back at one of the interesting decades of the twentieth century and how it impacted on the Manchester area in words and pictures - though many of the captions carry additional information. We have not attempted to cover everything – that would be impossible - but what is here just might tempt some of you to do a little digging into the past as there is plenty to go at. As with the other titles in the series, this is more a dib in, dib out, pull it all about publication. Look at the pictures, read the captions, agree or disagree and, if you are old enough, call up a memory or two of your own which you are welcome to share with us on the iNostalgia Facebook page. Above all enjoy.

Acknowledgements

Titles such as *Around Manchester in the 1970s*, would not be possible if it were not for the talents of the photographers and journalists of the *Manchester Evening News* and *Daily Mirror* and the archivists at Mirrorpix including: Tony Cordt, John Holland, Clive Cooksey, John Fowler, Brian Randle, Dezo Hoffman, Eddie Sanderson, John Walker, John Featherstone, Bill Batchelor, Ian Currie, Gerald Brown, Roy Spicer, Irene Shannon, Doreen Spooner, Chris Aspin, Barbara Duncan, Peter Gardner, Keith Ward, Jill Burdett, Beryl Jones, Peter Bainbridge, Matt D'Arcy, David Bainton, Neal Keeling, Chris Stewart, Janine Watson, John Trickett, Eric Thornton, John Kay, Tom Buist and Brian Hope. Also, special thanks to Simon Flavin and John Mead at *Mirrorpix*.

Out and About

Salford completed its first tower block – the eight-floor, 110-apartment, Clement Atlee House - in May 1956, and by the early 1960s had the first of its fifteen-storey blocks under construction. The city's largest development was at Kersal, where thousands of people were rehoused in local authority-owned tower blocks. Even so, as the 1970s dawned, much of the city's housing stock still comprised row upon row of terraces, of which a few were owner occupied. The majority were owned by private landlords.

Corrie's Stan and Hilda Ogden, alias Bernard Youens and Jean Alexander, paid a nostalgic visit to Archie Street, Salford, just before it was demolished in August 1971.

Demolition in progress in Openshaw, January 1971.

(Above left). Despite its rehousing programme, Salford, in October 1974, was said to have the worst slums in Europe. Here, Mrs Sloan and her five-year-old son Jeffrey inspect the damage following the collapse of part of a ceiling at their home.

(Above right and bottom left). Slum housing in Salford, January 1970.

(Above left and right). A typical backyard of the type many of us grew up with. A least the outside loo has lino on the floor.

(Opposite page). Children play in a back alleyway off Clifton Street, Ordsall, Salford. May 1970.

(Right). Singer, songwriter and keen photographer Vince Hill takes a break from rehearsals to record the changing face of Salford in February 1970.

At least someone is trying to keep the place clean.

Living the dream? This is the Passman family - mum Mary with sixteen-month-old Jacqueline and dad Robert. The date is November 1973 and the Passmans are tenants in the Hulme Crescents – in its day the largest public housing development in Europe aimed at accommodating 13,000 people. For many residents, the dream quickly turned into a nightmare thanks to serious design flaws and construction errors. There were problems with sewage disposal, central heating system failures, condensation, vermin infestation and totally inadequate waste collection. From being the flagship of social housing, Hulme took the native all-comers' record by being branded the worst public housing scheme in British history.

\ view across the rooftops of Salford. In the lower image, the floodlight towers of Old Trafford can be seen in the distance. Part of 'rafford Park and No.6 Dock are in the background on the right of the image. Both images date from July 1974.

We give
GREEN
SHIELD
stamps
Jellies
Weetabix
Discount
FAMILY-SIZE WEETABIX
11½p
DELIGHT 6p
Vesta
FLAN MIX 9½p
CONDENSED MILK
7p
TESCO
TOMATO JUICE
DISCOUNT!
9p

Cadbury's Cakes
ATORA
CUSTARD
HAM
HEINZ

(Above). The one-and-only Muhammad Ali (Cassius Clay) looked as exhausted as if he had just gone fifteen rounds with Joe Frazier. It was 12 October 1971, and Ali was making a personal appearance at the Tesco supermarket in Stretford, promoting Ovaltine. He was supposed to autograph the tins customers had bought, but the crush was such that Ali found himself sandwiched between the stacks. The police were called and the event cancelled.

(Opposite page top). By the early 1970s, supermarkets were well established throughout South Lancashire even if many were still on the small side. This image was taken in 1972 when prices were shown in both old and new money, such as Fussell's condensed milk 7p (1/5d) and Tesco tomato sauce 9d (1/9d). During the late 1970s, the *MEN* journalist Irene Shannon looked after the paper's Price Guide column, a weekly update of retail prices throughout Greater Manchester. After groceries, meat formed the most important – and usually most costly – part of household shopping budgets. Seven types of meat were included in the weekly surveys, the findings listing both the cheapest and most expensive. A typical list published on Monday 31 October 1977 stated that the most expensive lamb chops, at £1.20per pound, were in the west region (Wigan, Bolton and Leigh). The cheapest were to be found in Wythenshaw at 68p per pound, whilst in Oldham it was possible to buy sausages at 24p per pound. Customers in the west region were paying 52p per pound.

(Opposite page bottom). The date this picture was taken is not known though it was after decimalisation and before 3 February 1975. It was used in the *MEN* in April 1975 for a story on how some small grocers were taking on the discount supermarkets by offering all-round price cuts themselves. The picture is devoid of any discount labelling, special offer signs and so on, so it was probably taken for some other reason. Around the UK, the number of new town centre supermarkets was increasing rapidly (this is still in the days before out of town shopping malls). As a result, traditional corner shops and smaller grocery/general stores were finding it increasingly harder to compete on price. Even so, when compared to today's prices, the shelves are stocked with bargains: Knorr sauce mix 7p; large tins of Plumrose chopped ham 35p; Puffin pilchards 10p; Australian Gold apricots 23p and large Brown & Polson cornflour 17p.

(Above). Developed by Hammerson Investments and opened in 1965, Merseyway Shopping Centre, Stockport, was one of the first precincts in the UK. Hammerson opened the first covered mall in the UK in 1976 at Brent Cross.

(Below). Shoppers take a breather at the new Salford City Shopping Centre.

Customers browse around the new Salford City Shopping Centre. DER are offering TVs on free home trials and no deposit rentals, whilst at George Glass, one-size stretch tights can be had at 19p a pair, socks at 24p a pair and shirts for £1.39.

I WALK, TALK & SING
CHUCKLES
TIMPO WILD WEST CORRAL
TIMPO WILD WEST STAGE COACH
Clockwork Train Set
Clockwork Train Set
table tennis set
The Magic Sweet Shop
AURORA

(Right). CCTV security cameras come to Manchester. Due to high levels of shoplifting, the city's department stores began installing systems. December 1971.

(Opposite page). Christmas is coming. It is November 1970 and we are still in a time when toys were marketed either at boys or girls. About the only unisex items on offer are the latest Blue Peter book, a scooter, shuffleboard, and a couple of jigsaws. For girls, we have an ironing board and a selection of dolls including: "I'm Miss Ramella," Baby Beau and "I Walk, Talk and Sing." For the boys it's Airfix kits, train sets, and a range of Wild West stuff.

(Bottom). The January Sale begins early at Debenhams, Manchester. It is 29 December 1979 and the queue stretches in both directions along Market Street.

Facebook Memories

Jean Murray – I remember going to see Santa at Lewis's. One year my mum - I must have been nine years old - asked me what I wanted for Christmas. I told her that I had written my letter and sealed it and was going to post it and I would tell Santa at Lewis's to watch out for it as I had been very good. My mum was horrified. She had no idea what I had asked for but came up with a stormer. "Oh, I'd better let me check your spelling. Santa won't know what to bring if you've spelt it wrong."

The Old Shambles, incorporating the 600-year-old Wellington Inn and Sinclair's Oyster Bar, posed something of a problem for the Arndale Shopping Centre development architects Hugh Wilson and Lewis Womersley. The Shambles were amongst the last Tudor period buildings in the city centre and too important to be bulldozed, but the development required them to be raised to a new height of nearly five feet above their original levels. The remedy was to pour a massive concrete underpinning/new foundation, capable of supporting the buildings, whose combined weight was 470tons, and then raise them to the required height using hydraulic jacks.

Work on the American-style Arndale itself started in 1972 and it was constructed in phases over the following seven years. The Arndale Tower and sixty shops opened in September 1976, with the Knightsbridge Mall and Northern Mall opening in May and October 1977 respectively. The 200-stall Market Hall, Boots and the bridge to the Shambles were completed in 1978. Cannon Street bus station, British Home Stores and Littlewoods were added the following year.

RESTAURANT
OLD SHAMBLES
Sinclair's
GRILLS
AND ALL SEA FOOD
DINING ROOM UPSTAIRS
Grills

GRAVELEYS FROZEN FOODS
10/109-110 ARNDALE MARKET, MANCHESTER
JUST A FEW OF OUR
FANTASTIC ICE CREAM PRICES

GRANELLIS

17 oz block VANILLA 18p
17 oz block RASP RIP 20p
1 litre VANILLA.......... 40p
1 litre RASP RIP 44p
2 litre VANILLA.......... 75p
2 litre RASP RIP 85p
2 litre RUM RAISIN 99p
4 litre VANILLA £1.30
4 litre RASP RIP........ £1.50

PENDLETONS

10 MEXI CHOC.......... 55p
10 TWICER 55p
15 CHOC ICE 90p
20 DOUBLE FLAVOUR.... 60p
ARCTIC ROLLS.......... 28p
ICE POPS........ 20 FOR 18p

WE ARE ON BOTH
UPPER & LOWER MARKETS,
SO DO NOT FORGET!

KING HENRY'S
TWO WEEK SPECIAL
2 FREE MUFFINS
WHEN YOU BUY
½lb. OF COOKED MEAT
FROM OUR LARGE SELECTION

Crusty Cobs .... 19p each
Jam Ball Doughnuts....... 3 for 21p
Oven Bottom Muffins...... 4 for 15p

KING HENRY'S
UNIT 127, HIGH STREET MARKET,
ARNDALE CENTRE,
MANCHESTER.
(NEXT TO DON MILLERS)

ONLY THE BEST
IS GOOD ENOUGH
FOR YOU!

WE SUPPLY ONLY THE BEST
IN BACON, CHEESE
AND COOKED MEATS

DANISH CHEDDAR CHEESE 73p PER lb
FARMHOUSE CHESHIRE CHEESE 73p PER lb
DANELARD 10½p ½lb PKT
'FAYMOS' SOFT MARGARINE 15p 8oz TUB
COOKED SHOULDER HAM 19p PER QTR
P.G. TIPS TEA 21p PER ¼lb
HEINZ BAKED BEANS 13½p 15¾oz
BATCHELORS BIGGA PEAS 9½p 10oz

shop at
HUGH
FAY

ARNDALE RETAIL MARKET,
MANCHESTER

VISIT
B+J ASHTON'S
QUALITY
MEAT MARKET
STALL 17 & 18
LOWER MARKET HALL
(ENTRANCE AT HIGH STREET)

5 lbs. SCOTCH BRAISING STEAK .. £3.99
5 lbs. CHESHIRE PORK CHOPS £3.99
5 lbs. BEST BRAISING CHOPS £2.25
5 lbs. CHESHIRE BELLY PORK £1.75
BONELESS STUFFED BELLY PORK 45p lb.
NEW ZEALAND LAMB CHOPS (FRY OR GRILL) .... 89p lb.
LEAN MIDDLE CUT BACON ...... 62p lb.
CHESHIRE PORK JOINTS ..... 45p lb.
FRYING LIVER ..... 34p lb.
SCOTCH SHIN BEEF 69p lb.

ALL OUR MEAT IS
OF SUPERB QUALITY
TELEPHONE
061-834 3132

(Above). Market Street, Manchester, in April 1977, looking towards the Arndale Centre.

(Opposite page top). Construction work under way on the £100million Arndale development in 1974. In the top image, Market Street is on the left and the Old Shambles, at right foreground, are now hidden from view, protected from everyday knocks and scrapes by corrugated sheeting. When finally completed, Manchester's Arndale was the largest Arndale Mall complex built, accommodating 210 shops and 200 market stalls.

(Left). Watch out, watch out, there's static about. Brentford Nylons (The Money Savers) was one of the well-known names in 1970s retailing along with the likes of Woolworths, Boots, Radio Rentals, and Burtons. Brentfords offered a wide range of inexpensive blankets, bedspreads, sheets and nighties. Our image of the Manchester branch on Piccadilly Plaza is thought to date from February 1976, the year the company went bust in spectacular fashion only to be bought by Lonrho for a knock-down price. But for many, Brentford Nylons will forever be associated with sweaty nylon sheets, static electric shocks and disc jockey Alan 'Fluff' Freeman, who fronted their advertising campaigns.

WOOLWORTH
WOOLWORTH
WOOLWORTH
KINGSONIC

Comprising six floors and two basement levels, the Woolworths department store, Piccadilly Gardens, was the company's largest outlet in Europe. At around 1.30pm on 8 May 1979, a taxi driver contacted his control office reporting smoke coming from Woolworths – she dialled 999. Within a few minutes, the fire brigade had received twelve calls and appliances raced to the scene. Fire had broken out in the furniture department, the cause being a damaged electrical cable which ignited furniture filled with polyurethane. The fire spread quickly, the lighted polyurethane producing thick toxic smoke making it almost impossible to see. The types of foam used in furniture can quickly become flowing pools of burning liquid that produce toxic fumes in the form of cyanide gas. The store was not fitted with a sprinkler system and escape via upper floor windows was impossible as they were fitted with iron bars – the fire brigade had to send for specialist cutting equipment to remove them.

It was estimated that around 500 people had been in the store. Of these, nine shoppers and one member of staff were killed and forty-seven injured. Six firefighters were injured rescuing twenty-six people from inside the burning building. Most of those who died were found in the restaurant area, unable to make their escape due to the thick toxic smoke. The second floor was gutted and the third floor suffered severe smoke damage. It was the worst shop fire for casualties since the Second World War, and the city's greatest conflagration since Paulden's Department Store, Stretford, was destroyed on 8 September 1957.

There were positive outcomes from the Woolworths fire. The 1988 Furniture and Furnishings (Fire) (Safety) Regulations forced manufacturers to use non-flammable or, where appropriate, fire-retardant materials in furniture and cushions etc.

Piccadilly Gardens from the new NatWest office block in Fountain Street in July 1977.

MEN photographer Bill Batchelor took to the air in January 1974 to get this shot across central Manchester.

A tractor is called in to clear snow from pavements around Albert Square, January 1979.

The snow is snowing, Deansgate, Manchester, during 1978.

Smithfield Market 1973.

Facebook Memories

Comment Shudehill Market – I loved rummaging through the piles of books on Allen's stall at Shudehill. What a way to spend lunch hour. My passion was books by Mrs Henry Wood and Phillip Gibbs but for different reasons. By the 1970s many novels seemed to be written to a formula. Frankly it was becoming knickers off by the botttom of page five. With Mrs Henry Wood it was a case of spot the cad who would betray the heroine. Phillip Gibbs was in a class of his own. A distinguished journalist and official reporter during both world wars, he was prolific author writing on history and current affairs as well as novels. The thing about his novels was that some characters seemed to disappear as if he had either forgotten about them or didn't know what to do with them. During the 1920s, he also wrote screen plays for films.

And now for something on a completely different scale to Smithfield. This is the tiny open market and book lovers' paradise at Shudehill in May 1971.

Smithfield Market 1973, the union jack sack had last been used at the time of Queen Elizabeth's Coronation in 1953.

(Left). The Queen completes her walk along Spinningfields. The *MEN* offices are in the background.

(Below). Queen Elizabeth II chatting to the crowd in Spinningfields after opening the magistrates court building, Crown Square. 23 June 1971.

The bunting is up along Halliday Road, Newton Heath, and the royal motorcade makes its way along Grundey Street, Hazel Grove, during the 1977 Silver Jubilee Tour.

Youngsters from Cranberry Road, Gorton, enjoying the Silver Jubilee celebrations, 30 May 1977. Below, the bunfight is in full swing in Halliday Road, Newton Heath.

SILVER JUBILEE
MAJESTY
QUEEN ELIZABETH
25
25

(Opposite page). Maidstone Avenue, Chorlton. 7 June 1977.

(Left). *MEN* photographer John Holland was on hand to record for posterity thirteen-year-old 'Queen' Helen Taylor and three-year-old 'Princess' Amanda Riley with a Silver Jubilee street party celebration cake in Strawberry Hill, Pendleton. 7 June 1977.

Facebook Memories

M Hatters – There were about 200 people at our street party. People that I'd seen across the road, or taking their dog out, but never spoke to them. A great day.

(Above). Silver Jubilee celebrations in Millington Walk, Hulme.

(Left). Lord Mayor's procession passing in front of the town hall, September 1977.

World of Work

(Right). Timber is unloaded at No.9 Dock. August 1970.

(Bottom). No.9 Dock in August 1970. Manchester Liners' *Manchester Courage* is alongside the container terminal. Round-the-clock working enabled the 500-capacity containership to be turned around in just 48hours. The increase in container traffic resulted in No.8 pier being equipped with a 32ton derrick to handle vessels carrying part container loads. The vessel nearest the camera, alongside No.8 wharf, is Prince Line's *Spartan Prince*.

The view from the bridge of the *Manchester Crusade* as she takes on containers on 17 January 1972.

(Right). The view along No.9 Dock from No.2 Grain Elevator. The picture was taken in January 1974.

(Below). Where there's muck. Ever thought what happens every time you flush the loo? Most sewage from Manchester ends up at the Davyhulme Sewage Works, Europe's largest wastewater treatment plant. During the Sixties, a £6.2million modernisation programme equipped Davyhulme to handle 91million litres of sewage a day. The stuff left over after treatment is called sludge – and there is a lot of it to get rid of. Like other UK cities with access to the sea, disposal was simple. Load it on a ship, take it a few miles off land and dump it. This photograph was taken at Davyhulme by *MEN* photographer John Corfield in June 1972 for a story covering a strike action by their crews.

(Opposite page top). When it opened in 1923, Barton (employing 1673 workers) was one of the most advanced coal-fired electricity generating stations in the UK. Its location alongside the Bridgewater Canal enabled the coal – around 222,000tons a year - to be delivered by barge. In 1928, and again in 1938, additional generating sets were installed, enabling Barton to supply power across a wide area including the city of Manchester. The station closed on 18 March 1974, with demolition commencing in the late 1970s.

(Opposite page bottom). Trafford Park in the 1970s was in decline even though there was some investment from the oil industry. During the previous decade, the Park had seen closures including Lancashire Dynamo, Lancashire Wire and Truscon Cement. The seventies would witness the demise of others including the Co-op tea factory, British Trailer Co, the BSC steelworks (Taylors), the Superheater Co and the Burmah oil refinery.

(Below). In 1971, the British Steel Corporation (BSC) works at Irlam was under threat following a reassessment by BSC as to its future iron and steel making capacity. Irlam was a profitable integrated iron and steel making plant, whilst the works at Warrington specialised in carbon and mild steel wire-making. Despite it being profitable, BSC took the decision to stop iron and steel production at Irlam and sell the Warrington plant to Tinsley Wire Industries. Production ceased at Irlam, though the relatively new rod and bar mill remained open.

(Right). By the mid-1970s, the UK was suffering economically so it was something of a surprise when the Norwegian steelmaker Elkem-Spigerverket announced it was building a new plant in east Manchester. By January 1975, the new mill was under construction on a fourteen-acre site at Beswick. The three-phase project included state-of-the-art electric arc furnaces and a rolling mill. Former workers at Irlam Steelworks were sent to Oslo for training, as the initial phase would create 150 much-needed jobs in the area. When fully operational, Manchester Steel expected to employ 350 workers. Our image shows the first pour of fifty tons of molten steel on 30 August 1975.

(Bottom). The continuous caster operating at Manchester Steel in February 1978.

Demolition in progress at Irlam Steelworks, 1975. The rod and bar mill closed in 1979.

Margaret Thatcher presses the flesh as she arrives at the first new spinning plant in the Greater Manchester area in half a century - the new £6million Carrington Viyella factory at Atherton. Viyella merged with Carrington Dewhurst in 1970 and was 64per cent owned by ICI, though ICI took no part in its day-to-day operations. At the time of the merger, the new company had nearly 40,000 employees, but rationalisation soon came, with subsidiaries sold off and an announcement that twelve factories would close. Other Viyella and Carrington Viyella mills around Atherton included Howe Bridge Mills, Ena Mill and Laburnam Mill.

Owned by J P Coats & Co., Eagley Mills, Eagley, near Bolton, was scheduled to close in June 1972 with the loss of 600 jobs. On 27 November 1974, Rochdale MP Cyril Smith was able to raise the problems facing the Lancashire textile industry in an Adjournment debate – it was the first debate in the House on a UK county other than London in more than two years. Smith pointed out that textiles provided 30per cent of Rochdale's total employment – though many were working a four-day week. He also pointed out that since 1959 the total labour force in cotton and allied textiles had fallen from 240,000 to 88,000 and that the number of spindles had dropped from 17.5million to 2.7million.

Short-time working throughout the industry was a result of the high level of imports from developing countries and EEC members such as Italy. Imports of cotton and man-made fibres accounted for 57per cent of home consumption in 1973 and figures for the first six months of 1974 showed imports at 60per cent of home consumption.

A major cause for concern was the Turkish Government's high-level of subsidies to its growing textile industry allowing manufacturers to offer textiles at prices barely above production costs. Turkish imports were 30metric tons in 1972, but the figure for the first eight months of 1974 showed imports of 2,680metric tons. Since July 1974 there had also been an upsurge in imports of finished garments from Taiwan.

(Right). Manchester fashions. Female football supporters at Salford on their way to a match. 24 August 1972.

(Bottom right). Image from a *Daily Mirror* Manchester Fashion Spy article by Doreen Spooner, January 1978.

(Bottom left). Sue Dexter and Jane Powell (right) model outfits at a preview of a fashion show, part of the Manchester Festival, May 1973.

(Right). The end of an era and the end of a Manchester landmark came in August 1973 when the remains of NCB Bradford Colliery were demolished. Photographer John Featherstone went along to record the end of the 5000ton, 200ft high concrete and steel Keope winding tower above No.2 shaft. First, the supports were blasted away - then came the collapse. Once the dust had settled, a demolition team moved in and began clearing the rubble. NCB Bradford had provided coal direct to Stuart Street Power Station by means of an underground tunnel. Though there was plenty of high quality coal in the area, the geology was causing problems, with subsidence damage occurring in Bradford village and Miles Platting. The NCB estimated that for every ton mined, 5s 2d had to be paid out in compensation for surface damage, thereby making Bradford uneconomic. The pit, which employed 1500 workers, closed in 1968.

(Bottom). Miner Thomas Taylor stands amid the remains of NCB Nook Colliery. The colliery closed in 1965. The photograph was taken in June 1970.

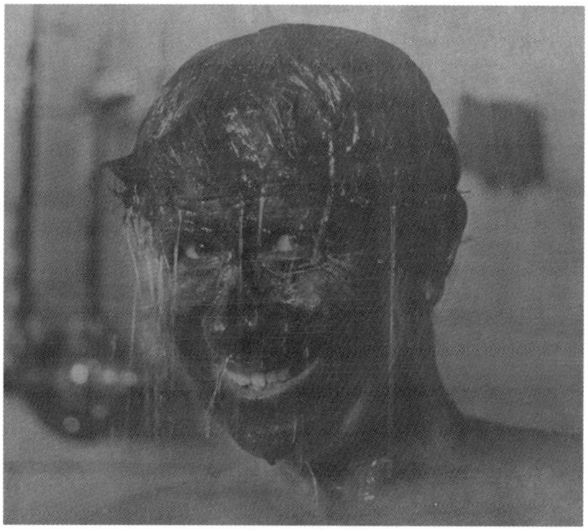

(Above). A miner scrubbing up after his shift at soon-to-be-closed NCB Astley Green Colliery, February 1970. On nationalisation, Astley employed 1375 underground and 561 surface workers, including women employed screening coal. The pit later became a mining museum.

(Top right). Miners at NCB Agecroft Colliery dismantle an electric motor.

On 18 March 1979, there was an explosion 1800ft underground at NCB Golborne Colliery, near Wigan, in which three miners were killed and eight critically injured – some suffering 90per cent burns to their bodies. Rescue teams converged on Golborne and striking ambulance workers called off their action to take the injured to hospitals. Two days after the disaster, it emerged that a ventilation fan had been out of order, resulting in a build-up of methane gas at a faster rate than normal. It also emerged that the pit management were aware that the fan wasn't working. By 2 April, the number of dead had risen to ten. The Mayor of Wigan started a fund, raising £30,000 to help dependents.

(Above). The Queen with Sir Cyril E Harrison, Chairman of the Board of Governors, United Manchester Hospitals, at St Mary's Hospital, 21 June 1971.

(Right). A typical early 1970s out-patients department of a local hospital – in this case Ancoats. The décor is still as bleak as it would have been in the Edwardian era, the only nod in the direction of modernity being the Nestles chocolate machine on the wall.

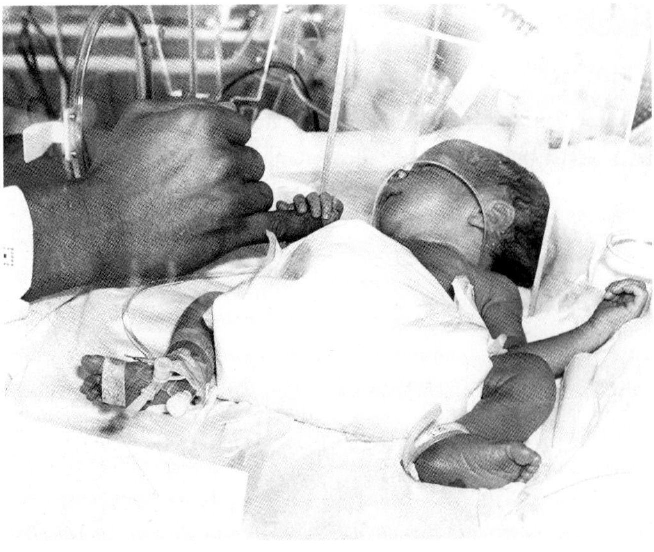

Britain's first test-tube baby Louise Brown holds on to her father's finger for the first time. Louise was the first baby to be conceived by invitro fertilisation (IVF), thanks to pioneering work by Patrick Steptoe and Robert Edwards, though in reality her actual conception took place in a petri dish. Louise was delivered at Oldham District General Hospital on 25 July 1978 by planned Caesarean section performed by registrar John Webster. Four years later, Louise's sister Natalie was also conceived using IVF.

(Previous page). Rochdale-born David Taylor was the first veterinary surgeon ever to extract a tooth from an elephant – he had to use a hammer and stonemason's chisel as no specialist equipment existed. It was this incident that would lead to him becoming first veterinary surgeon in the world to specialise in zoo and wildlife medicine. He also became a world-renowned expert on marine-mammals - and once prevented an orca (killer whale) from haemorrhaging to death by feeding it black pudding. He trialled and developed immobilizing drugs for large animals and was the first person in the UK to use a rifle for firing tranquilliser darts.

He once told me that when it came to an anaesthetic for an elephant, it was a matter of giving the animal enough to knock it out but not too much, as it was vital it was not lying on one side for too long. The reason being that the weight pressing down on the lungs causes a build-up of fluid and it will, in effect, drown. This is what happened to the elephant he extracted the tooth from. David kept the tooth on his desk, both as a memento and a reminder to him of the incident that changed his entire career. David's exploits were brought to our television screens in the 1980s in the BBC TV series *One by One*. The extraction of the elephant's tooth features in series one, episode two. David told me that the BBC special effects department made a lifelike elephant's head in which the original real tooth was inserted. The elephant being sedated in the TV series is for real and was due a real examination by David. "Everything had to go to plan," David told me, "The BBC special effects had made a lifelike elephant's head, but only the left side to save money. When I tranquilised the real elephant, it had to go down on its right side, otherwise viewers would be writing in. So the plan involved having several keepers on hand to push the elephant the correct way when it started to wobble."

Sid Groves, a foreman at Wilberforce Turner & Co, Salford, with the latest batch of candles. The firm had suddenly become very busy since the start of the power workers' work-to-rule. 9 December 1970.

After 48 years on the railway, wheel-tapper Joe Holtby handed in his hammer for the last time in November 1975. By 1975, Joe's trade was already a dying art on British Rail.

(Above). Comedy duo Tommy Cannon and Bobby Ball returned to the Crane Fruehauf factory, Oldham, where they had both worked as welders. October 1978.

(Right). Back in May 1973, Elsie and Jimmy Greenwood of Rochdale had one of the last operational coal-fired fish and chip fryers in Lancashire. At the beginning of the 1970s, fish and chips was still a relatively cheap way of feeding the family. I remember back in the late 1950s fish and chips costing 3d (1.5p) for the chips and 6d (2.5p) for the fish. A large potato fritter (scallop) cost 1d (0.5p) and scratchings – the bits of fried batter that had come off the fish - were free. Things went pear-shaped during the heat wave of 1976, which resulted in a shortage of decent potatoes for making chips. Prices rocketed and somewhat strangely never really dropped again once the shortage was over. The 1976 shortage led to potatoes being imported from around the world - and with some of them came second-mating blight which is still causing problems in 2017. However, there are still (2017) several coal-fired fryers in use, including Fields Fish Shop, Esh Winning, County Durham.

Strikes, Protests and Politics

(Right). A lone policeman stands watch on Manchester's deserted dockside on 8 December 1970.

(Bottom). A misty morning in December 1970 and all is quiet at Manchester Docks as the dockers are on strike. Among the nineteen ships standing idle is the Ellerman cargo-liner *City of Guildford*.

(Above). By the early 1970s, the increasing use of containerisation was seen by dock workers on both sides of the Atlantic as a serious threat to their livelihoods leading to strikes in both Montreal and Manchester.

(Right). A docker is led away by police during the strike at Manchester Docks in August 1972.

(Bottom). Among the ships caught on camera by *MEN* photographer John Holland on 21 September 1974 were the *Eskdale*, owned by Turnbull Scott Shipping Co and Ellerman Lines' *City of Glasgow*. The docks were at a standstill due to industrial action by dock workers and lock gatemen on the Manchester Ship Canal. The gatemen's strike was costing the canal company thousands of pounds a day and had effectively bottled-up 48 ships in the docks and at various places along the length of the canal. At least another fifteen ships were anchored on the Mersey Bar waiting to enter the canal system. In a separate dispute over demands for a shorter week, Manchester's 800 dock workers had walked off the job on 20 September.

In December 1970, power workers imposed a work-to-rule during a dispute over pay. This in turn led to power cuts, though these residents in Cherry Tree Lane, Stockport, could shed a bit of light around their living room thanks to the gas mantles on either side of the fireplace still working.

During the December 1970 power workers' work-to-rule, candles might have been fine for lighting homes, offices and retail premises but hospitals required a more robust approach. This 27Kv mobile generator was loaned by the Royal Artillery TAVR, Belle Vue, to Booth Hall hospital. It was capable of supplying lighting and power to two blocks and the burns unit. Deputy engineer Kenneth Hill, assisted by some interested children, fires up the beast.

Manchester & Area Electricity Control. This where all power cut decisions were taken during the work-to-rule by power workers. December 1970.

Post Office clerical workers on picket duty outside the Post Office telephone offices in Portland Street, Manchester, as the city's 25,000 members of the Civil & Public Services Union strike. On 30 October 1970, the CPSA submitted a pay claim for a £3 a week rise. Though not much by 2017 standards, this represented a rise of between 15-20per cent and, if implemented in full, would have cost £50million a year. On 14 January 1971, the management offered 8per cent which was rejected outright. Six days later, post office workers walked out beginning the first national strike in the union's history. The strike lasted seven weeks, though some post offices continued to open for a few hours each week for the payment of pensions and other benefits.

(Below). Strikers file into the Odeon Cinema in central Manchester to hear details of the proposed peace formula to end the strike. The deal, hammered out at the Department of Employment, offered 9per cent but with efficiency savings. The strikers voted 14-1 to accept it. The strike cost the Post Office an estimated £25million in lost business.

(Top and above right). An estimated 5000 people marched through Irlam on 21 May 1971, demonstrating at the threat by British Steel to run down and virtually close Irlam steelworks with the loss of 4353 jobs by 1974.

(Middle left). Workers at Irlam Steelworks prevent lorries entering the site during protests over British Steel's threat to run the plant down.

(Left). Herbert Morley, in charge of British Steel's General Steels Division, was forced to abandon his car and run a gauntlet – with a police escort – of more than 200 women protesting over the threatened closure of Irlam. Morley was at Irlam to hold talks with the unions over the future of the plant.

(Above). On 5 January 1972, *MEN* photographer John Featherstone was on hand at NCB Agecroft Colliery, Pendlebury, to record the last miners coming off shift prior to a national strike called by the NUM. The strike was called in protest following a pay-rise offer of just £2 a week. By mid-February, no less than fourteen power stations were off line due to both a lack of coal and overtime bans by power and railway workers. The NUM used around 15,000 flying pickets to successfully disrupt supplies throughout the country. The Conservative Government declared a state of emergency and introduced the three-day week so that power supplies could be rationed. Ironically, productivity hardly dropped as workers – especially those on piece work - pulled out the stops to do five day's work in three.

(Right). Striking miners picket Agecroft power station. January 1972. In all, from 1970-75, there were 16,708 strikes involving 8,620,000 workers.

(Right). The pickets have gone and it's all over bar the final vote. Agecroft power station main gate, February 1972.

(Bottom). More than 600 miners march through Manchester following the end of their strike. February 1972.

(Above). Rubbish piled high outside the Booth Street depot, Stockport, during the dustmen's strike in September 1976. The pile was so high it almost reached the sign 'Tipping of refuse prohibited'.

(Left). November 1977 saw the first ever national strike called by the Fire Brigades Union after rejection of a 30per cent pay rise claim. At the time, firefighters were paid £71.10p for a basic 48hr week (£3600 a year) at a time of rampant inflation and industrial unrest. Our image shows the firefighters' picket outside London Road Fire Station, Manchester, on 21 November 1977.

Facebook Memories

D Gill – I was in the RAF during the firemen's strike and was assigned to a Green Goddess in the Manchester area. Our crew was a mixture of RAF and army. One morning we were called out to rescue a cat stuck up a tree. We rescued Mr Fluffy and were invited to tea, cakes and biscuits by the old lady who owned him. She told us that during the war she had been a ferry pilot delivering aircraft to front line squadrons. She showed us her log books. She had flown all sorts of aircraft including Spitfires, Boulton-Paul Defiants, Hurricanes, Typhoons - even bombers. A great lady.

Fire cover during the dispute was provided by 10,000 servicemen manning four-wheel drive Auxiliary Fire Service Bedford RLHZ self-propelled pumps – better known as Green Goddesses due to their green paintwork. More the 900 Green Goddesses were built between 1953 and 1956. They formed part of the UK's civil defence force, their main role following a nuclear attack being to fight fires by pumping water from whatever source was available – stream, canal, ponds and so on. They had a top speed of 65mph, carried a single ladder, hoses and a pump. They were not fitted with radios and did not carry specialist equipment. They were mothballed in 1968, though kept in operational condition. During the strike, they were crewed by Army, RAF and RN personnel billeted at Territorial Army bases. Two soldiers were killed when a Green Goddess crashed at Newton Heath.

Striking Firefighters march through Manchester. The strike lasted nine weeks during which time fire damage cost the insurance industry £117.5million compared to £52.3million in the previous three months. Striking firemen left picket lines to tackle many fires, including a major outbreak at a London hospital. On 21 December, four children died in a house fire in Wednesbury, West Midlands, the first during the strike in which more than two people had died. Reporting the strike in the press was sporadic as the *Sun, Daily Mirror* and *Observer* had industrial problems of their own with striking print workers and journalists. The BBC was not immune either and was blacked out on 19 December due to a dispute over pay by engineers. The firefighters' strike was settled on 16 January 1978 when the Fire Brigades Union accepted a 10per cent pay rise.

Facebook Memories

Judith – Though not a pacifist I am against nuclear weapons. In the 60s and 70s word went around some CND members that if you wanted to find out if your phone was tapped don't pay the bill. The GPO wouldn't cut you off.

Sue – I ran a small bed and breakfast - a maximum of eight people could stay. One day I had a visit from Special Branch - I think. They asked if I had any Irish guests or bookings. Thatcher was due to visit the Manchester area.

The 12 January 1971 was a nationwide "Kill the Bill" day of action against the Industrial Relations Bill which included 1.5million members of the Amalgamated Engineering Union (AEU) staging a one-day strike. Introduced by the Conservatives, the Bill gave workers the right to decide if they wished to belong to a trades union but also reduced protection for workers, limited wild cat strikes and aimed to suppress the right to collective bargaining. Despite the protests, the Bill received its third reading in March 1971. Our image shows demonstrators marching through Manchester, including Hilary Creek and John Barker who were members of the Angry Brigade.

The Angry Brigade was a British libertarian communist terrorist group that came into being in mid-1968 during demonstrations outside the US embassy, Grosvenor Square, London, over US involvement in the Vietnam War. Some of the Brigade's members were former undergraduates at Cambridge. The Brigade was responsible for a series of bomb attacks carried out between August 1970 and December 1972 on the homes of Tory MPs as well as banks and embassies. One of the group's weirder attacks was the bombing of the BBC outside broadcast van assigned to the 1970 Miss World contest. The Government took the Brigade seriously and ordered the Met to smash it and arrests followed during March 1971. The tabloid press had a field day. The *Sun* managed to come up with the headline "Sex Orgies at the Cottage of Blood", the group allegedly engaging in anarchist meetings combined with bizarre sexual practices whilst sacrificing turkeys. You couldn't make it up – well you could.

In 1972, Hilary Creek, Anne Mendleson, Jim Greenfield and John Barker were tried and sentenced to fifteen-years apiece for their involvement, though their sentences were reduced following a plea for clemency from the jury.

And what of the Industrial Relations Act? It was one of the victims of Edward Heath's "Who Governs Britain?" General Election of February 1974. Two days before the election, the director general of the Confederation of British Industry, Campbell Adamson, made a speech in which he hoped the next government would repeal the Act. Many believe Campbell's speech scuppered Heath's chances. The incoming Labour Government repealed the Act.

(Risht). The file date for these photographs of a silent protest against British Army involvement in Northern Ireland is 31 January 1972. The day before, British paratroopers in Londonderry had fired on a civil rights demonstration against the internment of suspected Irish nationalists, killing thirteen and wounding seventeen others, in what became known as Bloody Sunday. In response, on 21 July, the IRA simultaneously detonated twenty devices in Belfast, killing many civilians and military personnel and began a bombing campaign on the British mainland. Among the high-profile victims were MP Airey Neave, killed by a car bomb, and Lord Mountbatten, killed when a device in his motor-launch detonated.

(Below). The trials of a Roman Catholic mother seeking contraception, abortion and welfare benefits were acted out in the streets of Manchester on 2 March 1973 by members of the Women's Liberation Movement. The street theatre, played out beside the Mancunian Way, Oxford Road, was followed by a march through the city centre to St John's Recreation Ground.

In January 1973, Prime Minister Edward Heath signed the Treaty of Rome taking the UK into the European Economic Community. Membership meant severing trade agreements with Commonwealth countries such as Canada, Australia and New Zealand. The Labour manifesto for the October 1974 General Election promised the voters a referendum – the first in British history - on continued membership with the question, "Do you think the UK should stay in the European Community?" The answer being a simple Yes or No.

In April 1975, Labour held a one-day conference on the forthcoming referendum. The party was deeply divided; Shirley Williams (pro-EEC) said "It's much better than we had feared, but not quite as good as we had hoped". Employment Secretary Michael Foot (anti-EEC) was convinced the then latest high unemployment figures were down to damage done to the domestic market by European imports. Though Conference voted two to one in favour of leaving, the government recommended staying in. Tabloids such as the *Sun* advocated a vote to stay in. The result was 67per cent in favour of remaining.

These images taken in St Peter's Square, Manchester, in April 1977 feature members of the Anti-Market League stating the case for another referendum on the UK's membership of the European Economic Community. Pressure groups opposed to membership of the EEC had formed as early as 1961 in response to the UK's failed attempt to join. The Anti-Market League favoured free trade with the world as a whole and not just the EEC. Unlike the 2016 referendum, the 1975 one was held in a civilised manner with both sides willing to listen to what the other had to say. No shouting down, no lies, no intimidation.

Anthony Barber had been the Conservative MP for Altrincham and Sale since winning the 1965 by-election caused by the elevation of Fred Erroll to the Lords. Following the 1970 General Election, Edward Heath awarded Barber the chancellorship of the Duchy of Cornwall, with responsibility for negotiating the UK's entry to the European Economic Community – better known these days as the EU. However, Barber had hardly got his feet under the table when the then Chancellor of the Exchequer, Iain Macleod, suddenly died. Barber was promoted Chancellor of the Exchequer. He is pictured here campaigning in Altrincham and Sale during the 'Who Governs Britain?' General Election in February 1974. Prime Minister Edward Heath called the election following a miners' strike and the Three-Day Week. The electorate returned a hung parliament and when coalition talks between the Conservatives, Liberals and Ulster Unionists failed, Labour leader Harold Wilson formed a minority government. A second election, called the following October, again returned Labour but this time with a majority of three seats.

Labour's Barbara Castle campaigning in Salford ahead of the February 1974 General Election. At the time, Salford returned two members, one each for Salford West and Salford East. Salford East was abolished at the 1997 general election. In February 1974, Salford West was retained by Stan Orme for Labour on 16,808 votes (51.3per cent) and Salford East by Frank Allaun for Labour on 14,426 votes (54.5per cent). Orme had held the seat since 1964 and Allaun since 1955. They were both returned in the October 1974 General Election.

Campaigning under way in Bolton ahead of the February 1974 General Election. Labour candidates Ann Taylor (Bolton West) and David Young (Bolton East) get ready to press the flesh. Both were returned to Westminster. Ann Taylor polled 17,857 votes; B H Watson (Conservative) 17,257 votes; J Fish (Liberal) 4392 votes and K Bernal (National Front) 348. In the October 1974 election, Taylor polled 16,967 votes; Rob Redmond (Conservative) 16,061; Philip Stefan Linney (Liberal) 5127 votes and W Roberts (National Front) 1070. David Young polled 21,920 in the February election compared to 20,068 by Tory R Baldwin. S B Lawrence (Liberal) secured 3603 votes and J Hamilton of the National Front 457. In October, Young was again returned on 21,569 votes. The Tory vote dropped, John Heddle polling 17,504. T J Akeroyd (Liberal) polled 5792 votes; G Booth (National Front) 1106, and Harold Smith of the More Prosperous Britain party 149.

(Left). Cyril Smith, Liberal MP for Rochdale. He was first elected to Parliament in the 1972 by-election following the death of the sitting Labour member John McCann. In February 1974, he was returned with an increased majority polling 25,266 votes. Labour's Lawrence Cunliffe polled 16,367 and Conservative candidate Lillian Green 7933. The National Front candidate Michael W Sellors polled 1885. The Liberals returned to Westminster with fourteen seats – an increase of eight on the previous parliament - having polled 6,059,519 votes. Smith was appointed Liberal Chief Whip in June 1975. He was also victorious in the 1979 General Election.

(Below). In October 1977, the police had invoked the Public Order Act 1936 to ban the National Front from marching through Hyde, though they allowed their leader Martin Webster to go solo, surrounded by 2500 of Greater Manchester's finest – so plenty of overtime there then lads. Two months earlier, the NF had marched through the predominantly immigrant Lewisham, carrying placards '*85% of muggers are black, 85% of victims are white*'. In the inevitable clash that followed, 270 police and 200 NF members were injured. Webster had also done porridge for knocking the Kenyan Prime Minister, Jomo Kenyatta, to the ground outside the Hilton hotel, London.

Actress and political activist Vanessa Redgrave canvassing as the Workers Revolutionary Party candidate during the 1978 by-election in Moss Side. Redgrave came fifth, polling 394 votes.

Looking somewhat ill at ease, Margaret Thatcher receives an affectionate pat on the cheek and best wishes from 78-year-old Annie Lett of Stretford during a visit to Manchester shortly before the 1979 General Election. The election, held on 3 May, saw the Conservatives returned with 339 seats. Labour won 269 seats and the Liberals eleven seats.

Prime Minister Margaret Thatcher in Manchester during her one-day visit to the north west on 31 August 1979. Since winning the 1979 general election, Thatcher had been determined to continue the cuts in public expenditure introduced by the Heath Government of 1970-74. She instructed her ministers to find departmental savings of at least ten per cent and up to twenty per cent, though, to their credit, Francis Pym and Geoffrey Howe were opposed to the severity of the cuts. Thatcher also wanted the size of the civil service reduced from 566,000 to 500,000 staff. As education secretary in Edward Heath's cabinet, Thatcher withdrew daily free school milk from 7-11 year olds earning her the title 'milk-snatcher'.

Getting Around?

On 28 October 1971, *MEN* photographer Eric Graham joined the 2500 or so people who took advantage of an opportunity to walk along an unopened two-mile section of the M602 urban motorway. This section of the dual three-lane motorway – the first of its type in Lancashire – had been completed two months ahead of schedule at a cost of £11million, though its construction had caused chaos around Eccles for more than two years. The contractors opened the motorway to walkers for four hours and in glorious sunshine it became something of a day out as families made the four-mile round trip from the Salford end, where there was single lane access. The barriers were then put back to await the official opening. The £30million M602 – officially known as the South Lancashire motorway - was constructed to offer an alternative route to the narrow Manchester-Liverpool road through Eccles, Patricroft and Peel Green which, for more than fifty years, had been an accident blackspot.

Construction under way on a new section of the M63.

General view of the M62 motorway as it descends into the Irwell Valley. 16 July 1977.

The best-selling British-built car of the decade was the Ford Cortina Mk III. Introduced in 1970, the redesigned Mk III looked larger than the Mk II but was, in fact, the same overall length though it was four inches wider. It came in 1300cc, 1600cc and 2000cc variants and featured improved secondary safety over earlier models. The Mk III underwent some redesign during 1973. The number two best seller was the Ford Escort, with the Mini at number three.

1,127,000 new cars were sold in the UK in 1970, despite the fact we were being taken for a ride by being charged 36per cent purchase tax on every vehicle. Foreign-built cars accounted for only 14per cent of the UK's new car market and Japanese cars were still something of a novelty, having first been imported in 1965. In fact, in the early 1970s, some people refused to buy Japanese cars because of the way the Japanese had treated prisoners of war. From 1970-72, purchase tax was reduced in stages to 25per cent, resulting in a boost in sales of new cars to 1.7million, though ominously for UK manufacturers, imports rocketed to 450,000 vehicles of which 30,000 were Datsuns.

One of the unsung cars of the 1970s was the small, square, squat, Enfield 8000 two-seater battery-electric urban vehicle. Designed by Konstantine Adraktas, the uniquely aerodynamic 8000 had an aluminium body and was powered by eight 6V battery monoblocks, giving a top speed of around 48mph and a range of 56miles. Aimed primarily at the low urban mileage market, it had a turning circle comparable to a London taxi and passed the Department of Transport crash tests with flying colours. There was no gear lever; reverse was engaged by flicking a switch. It was equipped with an on-board charger that kicked-in when freewheeling downhill.

Our image features *Sunday Mirror* reporter Roy Spicer who road-tested the 8000 in June 1975. At £2600 each, Enfield 8000s were not cheap and take-up was minimal. Production ceased in May 1976.

The Transport Act 1968 brought into being four large scale bus operators, one each for Merseyside, Tyneside, the West Midlands and one covering South East Lancashire/North Cheshire (SELNEC). Each operator's bus fleet was formed by amalgamating city and borough fleets in their respective areas. SELNEC officially came into being on 1 November 1969, its constituent fleets being those of Manchester, Salford, Stockport, Oldham, Rochdale, Bolton, Bury, Ramsbottom, Leigh, Ashton and SHMD (Stalybridge, Hyde, Mossley and Dukinfield). SELNEC took over 2514 buses and, on 11 March 1970, unveiled its new livery - a deliberately politically neutral one of sunglow yellow/mancunian white (off-white). On the formation of the Metropolitan County of Greater Manchester in 1974, SELNEC changed its name to Greater Manchester Transport (GMT). This image shows former Ashton-under-Lyme No.43 sporting SELNEC livery. (Courtesy Clive Hardy).

Following the closure of Manchester Central station, passenger trains for the north were concentrated at Victoria, those for the south at Piccadilly, and, as there was no direct rail link between them, SELNEC ordered a fleet of 43 minibuses, the majority of which operated on the connecting service. The photograph shows one of the buses at Piccadilly. (Courtesy Clive Hardy).

A touch of the Continent came to the streets of Manchester in September 1978 when a 60ft long single-deck Volvo bendi-bus went on trials. John Brownhill, GMT group development engineer, test drove the vehicle. "At first, I was wary about the tail section swinging about, but you quickly realise that it follows the line perfectly. It is more predictable in its handling than an articulated trailer". The GMT had no policy on the use of bendi-buses but took the opportunity to test one as it could carry more passengers than the normal double-decker. At the time of the test, this type of bus could not legally be used in revenue-earning traffic, though a change in legislation was on the cards.

Members of Lancaster University Transport Society were at Oxford Road station on 30 April 1971 to see off one of the last of the Altrincham line's 1500V DC electric trains. Over the following weekend, BR engineers converted the line to 25,000Ac volts, bringing it into line with most of the network. Along with the changeover came new rolling stock.

A Hadfield-bound train on the 1500V DC line to Hadfield/Glossop. Electrification of the LNER's Manchester – Sheffield – Wath route began in the late 1930s but was abandoned following the outbreak of World War II. British Railways continued with the project and electric trains began running on 14 June 1954. The train seen here at Guide Bridge in the 1970s was designed by the LNER in 1938. This was the last 1500V DC line on BR and was converted to 25KV AC in late 1984. The units were maintained at Horwich Works. (Clive Hardy).

This three-car diesel multiple unit (DMU) was on show at Manchester Piccadilly at the beginning of September 1974 to test public reaction to BR's proposed DMU refurbishment programme involving 2000 vehicles. The programme included the complete refurbishment of vehicle interiors, new upholstery, fluorescent lighting and new floor coverings. The unit sported the Greater Manchester Transport logo to be carried by trains allocated to local services.

Hundreds of enthusiasts gathered at Salford and Manchester Victoria stations to watch a grubby looking *Flying Scotsman* on its way from Liverpool to Derby Locomotive Works for overhaul following repatriation from the US.

In 1969, *Flying Scotsman* went on a tour of major US and Canadian cities, hauling an exhibition train promoting British business. All was going well until some halfwit at our own Board of Trade (BoT) decided that perhaps an old steam locomotive was presenting the wrong image, whereupon the BoT set about undermining the venture by actively discouraging businesses from taking part.

The opportunity for *Scotsman* to earn her keep hauling fare-paying passengers was poor as she was prohibited from doing so by US law. As losses mounted, Scotsman's owner Alan Pegler moved her to San Francisco to take part in British Week. All went well until other exhibitors complained that the locomotive and her carriages were taking up nearly 100 car parking spaces. The train was moved further along Fisherman's Wharf and this proved disastrous as American visitors appeared either unable, or simply could not be bothered, to walk a few hundred yards.

Alan Pegler was left so broke that he had to work his passage home as an entertainer on a P&O liner. However, he was such a hit with the passengers that P&O offered him a full-time job. Before he left the US, Pegler found secure storage for *Scotsman* at an army base. The story might have ended there with creditors seizing the locomotive and selling her for scrap. Within hours of hearing of *Scotsman's* plight, enthusiast William 'Bill' McAlpine was organizing a rescue package. He arranged to buy the engine and discreetly paid off all known creditors. On 19 January 1973, *Flying Scotsman* was loaded onto the *MV California Star* at Oakland Docks, bound for Liverpool via the Panama Canal.

A suburban service approaches Manchester Piccadilly, 1974.

Apart from three engines operating on the narrow gauge Vale of Rheidol Railway, British Rail had withdrawn its steam locomotives from service in August 1968. However, for a few years after this, steam locomotives could still be found working at collieries, quarries, docks and power stations. One of the last locations in the Manchester area was Agecroft Power Station, where *Agecroft No.3* was still shunting wagons in 1973. (Courtesy Clive Hardy).

Trains in trouble No.1. Taken near Hadfield in May 1970, on the freight-only, Manchester Victoria-Sheffield Victoria Woodhead route. Gorton-built electric locomotive E26053 was hauling a heavy coal train when it ran away.

(Opposite page bottom). The Manchester Ship Canal Company operated one of the largest private railways in the UK with several hundred miles of sidings and connecting running lines. This is one of the company's locos shunting at Barton Wharf in 1971. (Courtesy Clive Hardy).

Train in trouble No.2, but this time we are at Dunham Massey, Altrincham, in September 1972, when this coal train derailed near the Rope and Anchor Hotel, chewing up 100yards of track in the process.

(Opposite page top). Trains no more No.1. On 24 February 1972, *MEN* photographer Tony Cordt visited Helmshore station on the former line from Stubbins Junction to Accrington, where he met up with Walter Baker, secretary of the East Lancashire Railway Co. In August 1969, the Helmshore and District Railway Preservation Society had opened a small museum at the station. At the time, the track was still in situ even though the station had closed completely on 5 December 1966. The society had then formed the East Lancashire Light Railway Co with the intention of reopening the line from Stubbins Junction to Haslingden Grane Road. However, before the ELLR could get the project off the ground, BR came along in October 1971 and ripped up the track. The outcome was that the group moved to Bury, forming the East Lancashire Railway. Out of this fledgling idea would come the North-West Museum of Science and Industry.

(Opposite page bottom). Trains no more No.2. This was the scene that greeted *MEN* journalist Gerald Brown and photographer Tony Cordt when they visited the derelict Didsbury station in March 1974. Didsbury had been one of the stations on the former Midland main line between Manchester Central and Derby, and was one of the victims of the ill-advised Labour minister of Transport Barbara Castle and not, as is widely thought, the Beeching Report. The last train to call at Didsbury had been the 1845hrs Manchester Central-London St Pancras service on 1 January 1967 with the station officially closing completely the following day. The station buildings were eventually demolished during 1981.

(Below). Trains no more No.3. Taken in August 1978, the former Manchester Central station had been reduced to a car park. (Courtesy Clive Hardy).

This image was taken by *MEN* photographer Clive Cooksey in June 1979, just over a year after a group of enthusiasts had banded together to acquire and restore Liverpool Road station - the oldest surviving passenger railway station in the country. Clive stood on the first railway platform in the world to get the shot. The station now forms part of the North-West Museum of Science and Industry.

Returning to Manchester in September 1979 was the 106-year-old steam locomotive *Penda*. Built by Beyer, Peacock & Co, Gortor in 1873 for the Isle of Man Railway, *Penda* had been donated to the fledgling North-West Museum of Science and Industry.

Former single-deck Californian-type Manchester tram No.765 in service at Crich Tramway Museum. The old car ran on the 53 service between Cheetham Hill Road and Brooke's Bar on Stretford Road, until withdrawn from service in 1929. No.765 then spent several decades as a farmer's shed until being rescued and restored by Manchester Transport Museum Society.

By the mid-1970s, horse-drawn vehicles were a rare sight in city centres. Here rag-and-bone man Russell Woods and his nag take five.

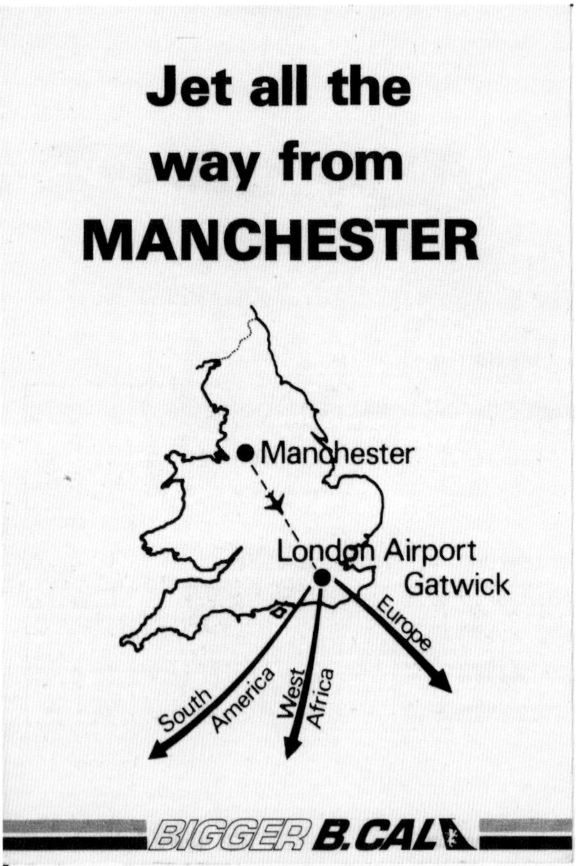

MANCHESTER – LONDON

Days of Operation	MONDAY TO FRIDAY			SAT		SUN	
Flight No. Aircraft Class	BR/UK 982 B11 Y	BR/UK 990 HLD Y	BR/UK 992 B11 Y	BR/UK 982 B11 Y	BR/UK 994 HLD Y	BR/UK 982 B11 Y	BR/UK 996 HLD Y
MANCHESTER (Ringway) dep.	0840	1130	1800	0840	2010	0840	1730
LONDON (Gatwick) arr.	0930	1240	1850	0930	2120	0930	1840

LONDON – MANCHESTER

Days of Operation	MONDAY TO FRIDAY			SAT		SUN	
Flight No. Aircraft Class	BR/UK 981 B11 Y	BR/UK 985 B11 Y	BR/UK 991 HLD Y	BR/UK 981 B11 Y	BR/UK 987 HLD Y	BR/UK 981 B11 Y	BR/UK 991 HLD Y
LONDON (C.L.A.T.) Check-in	0600	1500	1800	0600	1700	0600	1800
LONDON (Gatwick) dep.	0730	1640	1930	0730	1830	0730	1930
MANCHESTER (Ringway) arr.	0820	1730	2040	0820	1940	0820	2040

BIGGER B.CAL

The first ever BOAC Boeing 747 Jumbo jet to land at Ringway. August 1970.

Air travel increased in popularity during the early 1970s due in part to more and more Brits taking package holidays. During 1972 no less than 8.5million of us took a holiday abroad, mainly to Spain, France, Belgium and Austria, though there were adventurous souls who were going as far as Greece and Turkey. A consequence of increased air travel was the continuing development of Ringway, including extending the runway to 2745metres which enabled flights bound for Canada to take off fully loaded. By the end of 1978, Manchester had been classed as a category A international airport – the only one in the UK outside London - and fifteen airlines were operating scheduled services to thirty-seven destinations in the UK, Europe and North America.

The airconditioned intercontinental pier shortly after commissioning in 1974. Designed to handle Boeing 747s, these piers were the first to be equipped with air-bridges connecting passengers direct to aircraft.

On 3 July 1970, Dan Air flight 1903 from Manchester to Barcelona crashed into the wooded slopes of the Serralada del Montseny, Catalonia, killing all 112 passengers and seven crew. It was the deadliest civil aviation accident of 1970 and Dan Air's first involving fare-paying passengers. On 19 May 1973, an inbound Dan Air flight from Spain to Manchester experienced a failure with its nose-wheel landing gear and was diverted to RAF Manston, where it safely landed. Passengers escaped by way of the emergency exit chutes. The aircraft never flew again. It was sold to the MOD and used for SAS training.

On 7 January 1975, a British Airways BAC 1-11 airliner on a routine flight between Manchester and Heathrow was hijacked by an Iranian armed with a gun and explosives. The plane landed at Heathrow and the hijacker agreed to allow the passengers to disembark on the understanding that he would be flown to Paris. After refuelling, the plane took off but landed at Stansted where the hijacker was arrested. His gun turned out to be a toy and his explosives imitation.

There's something of an international flavour about No.9 Dock in this image dating from June 1978. On the left, just arrived from Pyreas, Athens, is the Dubrovnik-registered *Korcula*, whilst on the right we have the *Aegidia*, arrived from Bombay and forward of her is the *Clan Grant*, arrived from South Africa. In the foreground is the *Silver Arrow II* on a ferry service.

Ferries crossed the Manchester Ship Canal at many locations and for decades they had gone about their work with little or no publicity. That changed on 14 April 1970. On workdays, the ferry between Lock Lane, Irlam, and Bobs Lane, Cadishead, operated from 5.00am until late at night and this day was no different. Ferryman Bernard Carroll had made a couple of crossings and each time there had been an unpleasant smell coming off the canal. He decided to suspend the service and contacted the police. Whilst he was doing this, several passengers fearing they would be late for work commandeered a rowing boat and started crossing the canal. They were overcome by the fumes and soon in trouble, whereupon Bernard set off to help them. When he was about twenty feet from them, both boats were suddenly engulfed in a sea of fire as the very canal waters appeared to explode. Explosions continued to rock the area forcing the emergency services to evacuate nearby houses. Bernard and five others died in the inferno.

Subsequent investigations found that overnight the tanker *Tacoma* had taken on 1800tons of petrol at Partington Coaling Basin. Part of the safety regime required that two Shell employees had to be stationed on the quayside to watch for any spillage into the canal. The two men assigned to the task later admitted they spent four hours in the canteen during which time an estimated 14,000gallons of petrol had leaked into the canal. What caused the fire remained a mystery, though the possibility that someone had lit a cigarette remained firm favourite.

With the ferry out of action, workers travelling between Irlam and Cadishead faced an eight-mile detour.

(Opposite page top). By June 1971, the water level in the Rochdale Canal at Ancoats was so low that children could paddle in it in relative safety.

(Opposite page bottom). Derelict lock gates on the Rochdale Canal. The view is looking towards central Manchester from Castlefield.

(Right). It is January 1974, and work is under way clearing junk from the Rochdale Canal.

(Below). UMIST students Tim Noakes and Ian McCarthy check a set of refurbished lock gates.

You're Not Singing Anymore…

Bolton Wanderers

(Right). Bolton Wanderers' keeper Alan Boswell punches the ball clear of Sunderland's Billy Hughes during the league match at Roker Park on 3 October 1970. Sunderland opened the scoring in the tenth minute with a goal from Ian Porter. Three minutes into the second half, Paul Fletcher equalised for the Trotters, but in the 81st minute Gordon Harris put Sunderland 2-1 up. Four minutes later, Bobby Park made it 3-1 and two minutes after that substitute Joe Baker added Sunderland's fourth.

The season had started well with Bolton taking five points from their August fixtures. However, their five league fixtures in September brought just three points – an away win at Blackburn Rovers and an away draw at Sheffield Wednesday. October was slightly better with five points from six games, though the Trotters were knocked out of the League Cup in a Third Round replay at Leicester City. During November, the Trotters had just four league fixtures, managing to win one, draw one and lose two.

Not bad considering all was not well on the management side. Nat Lofthouse was no longer team manager; Jimmy McIlroy had taken over at the beginning of the month. Jimmy's stay was short-lived, resigning on 19 November after being told by the board to sell players. Bolton were effectively rudderless, losing at Carlisle United on Boxing Day, crashing out of the FA Cup Third Round at York City on 2 January and losing 3-1 at Orient on 9 January. Jimmy Meadows was appointed manager on 13 January and three days later the Trotters beat Sheffield United 2-1 at Burnden Park. Unfortunately, Meadows could not stop the decline in Bolton's fortunes. The side lost all its February fixtures, took three points from four games during March, took just one point from six games in April and drew the last match of the season 1-1 at Oxford United. Bolton had played 42 league fixtures, winning seven, drawing ten and losing the remainder. They were bottom of the Second Division and, for the first time in their history, Bolton Wanderers, one of the original founder members of the Football League, were relegated to the Third Division. Fellow founder members Blackburn Rovers were also relegated

(Bottom right). Bolton's Roy Greaves and Rochdale centre half Arthur Marsh in a heading duel during the Third Division fixture of 17 March 1973. The Trotters went on to win 2-1 and though they lost their last two games of the month, they went on the take the 1972-73 Third Division title. It was thanks to a superb run during April, in which they took twelve out of a possible fourteen points. Bolton finished on 61 points, four points clear of Notts County and six points clear of third-placed Blackburn Rovers. Interestingly, all three teams were original founder members of the Football League.

Arthur March joined Rochdale from Bolton in 1971 and in 1974 he moved to Darlington. Roy Greaves started his football career as a junior at Bolton, scoring twice in his league debut against Southampton. Though a striker, Jimmy Armfield moved Roy to midfield. Roy made 495 league appearances for the Trotters, scoring 66 goals.

Paul Jones (left) and Garry Jones during a pre-season training session at Burnden Park, July 1972. Paul Jones joined Bolton as an apprentice in July 1969, making his League debut on 17 January 1971 against Sheffield United. Originally a midfielder, he soon formed an outstanding defensive partnership with Warwick Rimmer, moving over to centre-half when John Hulme lost his first team place and went on loan to Notts County. Paul was the only member of the first team to play in every match during Bolton's Third Division title-winning season. He played 441 League games for Bolton, scoring 38 goals. During the 1980s, he had spells with Huddersfield Town, Oldham Athletic, and Blackpool.

Garry Jones had joined Bolton as an apprentice in 1966, making his League debut during the 1970-71 season. On 3 October 1971, he scored a hat-trick, including a penalty, during Bolton's 3-0 win over Manchester City in the Third Round of the League Cup. Injured towards the end of Bolton's Third Division title winning season, Garry lost his first team place to Neil Whatmore and spent part of the 1974-75 season on loan to Sheffield United. He returned to the first team for the 1975-76 season, making 36 League appearances, six FA Cup appearances and one League Cup appearance, scoring a total of thirteen goals. He again lost out to Steve Taylor and Frank Worthington and joined Blackpool in November 1978.

Above). 21 April 1973. Bolton are at home to York City and 20,062 fans are at Burnden Park for the whiff of promotion is in the air. A goal from Pete Nicholson and two more from Stuart Lee gave Bolton the points and the fans went wild. The Third Division title was secured with a 2-2 draw away to Port Vale and a 2-0 home win against Brentford on 23 and 28 April respectively

Players are mobbed by jubilant fans at the end of the match against York City. It was Division Two here we come.

Dressing room celebrations following the game against York City.

(Above). On 19 April 1976, fourth-placed Bolton were at Roker Park facing Second Division leaders Sunderland. Here, Sunderland's Tony Towers sends Bolton keeper Barry Siddall the wrong way. Bolton lost 2-1. Barry Siddall began his career at Bolton, making 137 appearances before moving to Sunderland in 1976.

Bolton Wanderers' winger Willie Morgan (left) and Chelsea's David Hey go head-to-head for the ball during the Second Division match at Burnden Park on 27 March 1976. Willie started his career at Burnley in 1960, moving to Old Trafford in 1968. He made 236 appearances for United, scoring 25 goals but lost his regular first team place to Steve Coppell. In 1975, he returned to Burnley, making sixteen appearances before moving on to Bolton Wanderers in 1976. He made 154 appearances for the Wanderers, scoring ten goals. Like many other players in the 1970s, he spent several summers on loan to US teams. In 1980, he moved to Blackpool.

Defender Sam Allardyce signed for Bolton from Dudley Town in 1969, making his senior debut in 1971. Sam made 184 League appearances for the Trotters, scoring 21 goals. He was transferred to Sunderland in 1980.

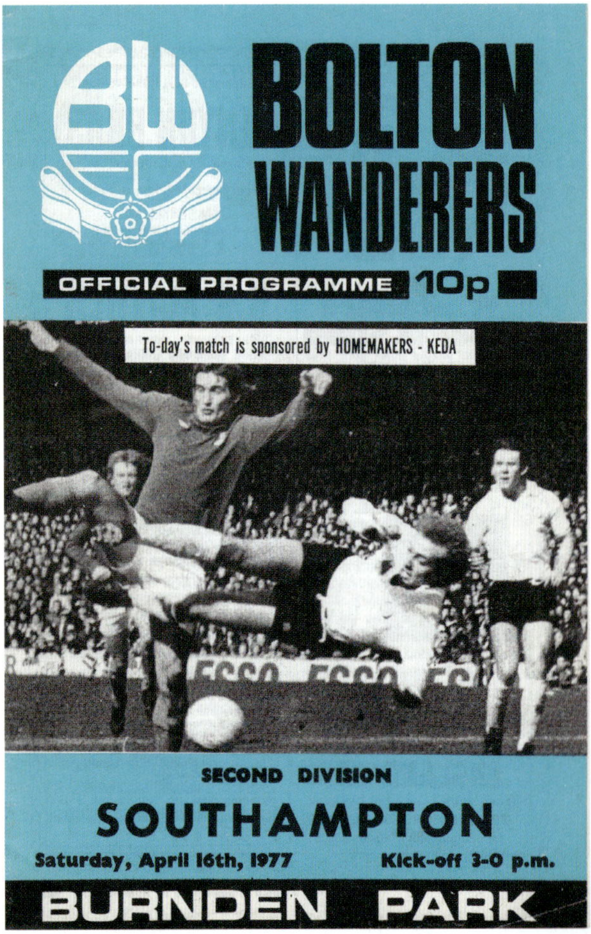
BOLTON
WANDERERS
OFFICIAL PROGRAMME
10p
To-day's match is sponsored by HOMEMAKERS - KEDA
SECOND DIVISION
SOUTHAMPTON
Saturday, April 16th, 1977
Kick-off 3-0 p.m.
BURNDEN PARK

When Bolton clashed with Southampton at The Dell on 22 October 1977, there was everything to play for. Both sides had played eleven League fixtures: Bolton were top of the Second Division having won eight, drawn two and lost one. The Saints were lying third, having won seven, drawn one and lost three. Tensions were running high and in our images Saints' striker Peter Osgood can be seen throwing a wobbly after being flagged offside. Phil Boyer is being restrained by Bolton players – he was still booked for retaliation. The match ended 2-2. Bolton led the Division on 19 points. Spurs were second on 17 points and Southampton third on 16 points.

(Opposite page, top left). Right-back Peter Nicholson beats Blackpool's Bob Hatton to the ball during Bolton's away tie on 12 March 1977. Peter Nicholson began his career at Carlisle United, moving to Blackpool in August 1969. He was the first player bought by Bolton manager Jimmy Armfield and went on to make 370 appearances between 1971-82.

(Opposite page, bottom left). Left-back David Burke signed for Bolton in 1977, making his League debut on 2 September 1978 in an away fixture against Birmingham City. He made 69 League appearances for the Trotters, scoring one goal. He was transferred to Huddersfield Town in 1981.

(Opposite page, bottom right). During his eight years at Burnden Park, Peter Reid made 225 League appearances for Bolton, scoring 23 goals. He was transferred to Everton in 1982.

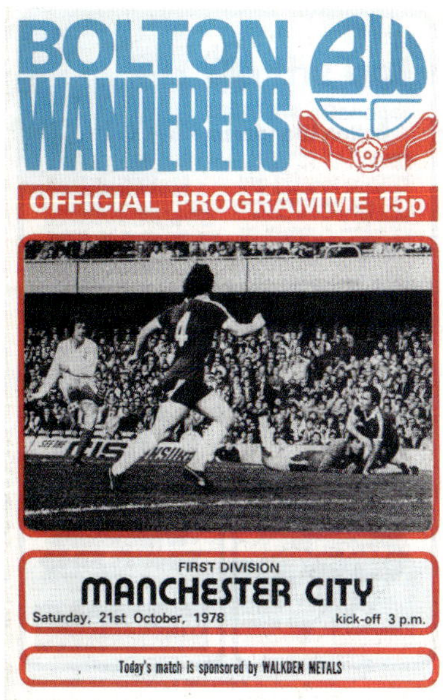

Manchester City FC

The 1969-70 League Cup competition was the first in which all 92 League clubs took part. The Fifth Round, played on 29 October, was a home tie and 42,058 fans turned up to see City earn a place in the semi-finals by beating QPR 3-0, thanks to two goals from Colin Bell and one from Mike Summerbee. The Semi-Final, against arch-rivals Manchester United, was played over two legs, the winner going through on aggregate. The first leg, played at Maine Road on 3 December, attracted 55,799 fans and ended with City winning 2-1. The second leg, at Old Trafford on 17 December, attracted 63,418 fans. It ended 2-2, City going through 4-3 on aggregate to meet West Bromwich Albion in the final at Wembley on 7 March. Our image shows West Bromwich Albion defender Doug Fraser beating Francis Lee to the ball.

Action from the 1970 League Cup Final. Only three days earlier, City had played their European Cup-winners' Cup, Third Round, 1st leg tie against Academica Coimbra in sunny Portugal and now here they were amid the snow and mud of Wembley in their first ever League Cup Final. West Brom opened the scoring in the sixth minute when Jeff Astle headed in a centre from Ray Wilson. It was fifteen minutes into the second half before City equalised, thanks to an unmarked Micky Doyle converting a corner kick that had involved Glyn Pardoe, Mike Summerbee and Colin Bell. 1-1 at full time, the game went into extra time. The winning goal came after twelve minutes when Francis Lee chipped the ball forward to Colin Bell, who then back-headed it to Glyn Pardoe who put it past West Brom keeper John Osborne.

City skipper Tony Book gets his hands on the famous three-handled trophy. The Seventies saw the competition dominated by five clubs, each of them winning it twice. Manchester City in 1970 and 1976; Tottenham Hotspur in 1971 and 1973; Wolverhampton Wanderers in 1974 and 1980; Aston Villa in 1975 and 1977 and Nottingham Forest in 1978 and 1979. The odd year out was 1972 when it was won by Stoke City.

29 April 1970 found City playing in their second final of the year – this time it was the European Cup Winners Cup Final against Polish side Gornik Zabrze in Vienna. Both teams had qualified by winning their respective 1968-69 season national cups – City beating Leicester 0-1 in the FA Cup, Gornik Zabrze beating Legia Warsaw 2-0 in the Polish Cup Final.

For City, George Heslop stood in for Mike Summerbee who was injured and Ian Bowyer was substitute. City opened the scoring in the 12th minute when Gornik's keeper Hubert Kostka managed to parry a thunderous shot from Francis Lee only for the ball to land at the feet of Neil Young who tapped it in. Our image shows Neil turning away to celebrate.

In the 23rd minute, Ian Bowyer came on for injured Mike Doyle and City changed tactics with Colin Bell moving deeper. In the 43rd minute, Neil Young found himself with only Kostka to beat. Kostka however had other ideas and charged off his line and upended Young. The referee had no hesitation in awarding a penalty which was put away by Francis Lee. In the 68th minute, Stanislaw Osilizio pulled one back for Gornik, the match ending 2-1 to City.

City manager Joe Mercer and skipper Tony Book hold the cup aloft during the victory parade through Manchester. To reach the final, City had beaten Athletico Bilbao, Lierse, Academica Coimbra and Schalke. Gornik had disposed of Olympiacos and Glasgow Rangers, but their legs against Levski Spartak ended 4-4 and they went through on the away goal rule. Their semi-final legs against Roma ended 1-1 and 2-2 and the subsequent replay ended 1-1. As there was no sudden death penalty shootout, Gornik went through on the toss of a coin.

Midfielder Colin Bell made 394 League appearances for City, scoring 117 goals. He made a further 90 appearances in FA Cup, League Cup and European Cup matches, scoring 35 goals, as well as winning 48 caps for England. On 12 November 1975, during a League Cup clash against United at Maine Road, Bell received a serious knee injury when he tangled with Martin Buchan. Returning during the 1977-78 season, he struggled to regain form and in August 1979 he announced his retirement. (Below). City legends Mike Summerbee and Francis Lee pose for the Press in March 1970.

(Above). City players close in on Arsenal's Alan Ball during the First Division match in front of 44,213 fans at Maine Road on 4 March 1972. Francis Lee scored both goals in City's 2-0 win.

Colin Bell looks on as Denis Law and Wolves' John McAlle battle for the ball. Five minutes before time, John Richards scored the winner for Wolves. It was Wolves' first major trophy since winning the 1960 FA Cup.

23 March 1974 and City are at Highbury facing the Gunners. The match entered sporting history. Not for the game itself which Arsenal won 2-0, but because it was the scene where the first instance of streaking in English football took place. John Taylor ran around the field stark naked until stopped by three policemen, who eventually forced him into a pair of trousers. Taylor was removed from the ground and finished up being fined. Streaking was already well established around US college campuses, though in 1973 a girl had streaked at a Los Angeles Kings ice hockey match. Some guy had also streaked across the Augusta golf course in Florida only to have his backside peppered with buckshot. The first streak at a major sporting event in the UK came on 20 April 1974 at an England v France rugby union match at Twickenham.

Rodney Marsh beats the Gunners' David O'Leary to the ball during City's 3-2 away win at Highbury on 4 October 1975. City were enjoying a bit of a roll, having beaten Stoke City 1-0 on 24 September, drawn 2-2 with United on 27th and stuffed Norwich City 6-1 in their League Cup Second Round replay on the 29th.

(Opposite page). Action from the League Cup Fourth Round tie against United at Maine Road on 12 November 1975. Two goals from Dennis Tueart and one apiece from Asa Hartford and Joe Royle put City through to the Fifth Round against Mansfield Town. The 4-2 victory over the Third Division club earned City a place in the semi-finals – a two-leg affair against Middlesbrough. City lost the first leg 1-0 but in the second destroyed the Teessiders 4-0 at Maine Road, going on to meet Newcastle United in the final.

TRUMANNS
ESSO
YOUNGERS

TRUMANNS
STEEL
PAINTS
YRES
YOUNGERS

The 1976 League Cup Final and City take on Newcastle United at Wembley. Here Peter Barnes bursts through a four-man wall of Newcastle defenders to open the scoring for City in the 11th minute. The move had started from a free-kick taken by Asa Hartford. The ball found skipper Mike Doyle who headed it across the goal where it was intercepted by Barnes.

In the 35th minute Newcastle's Alan Gowling put the ball past Dave Watson and keeper Joe Corrigan to make it 1-1.

City skipper Mike Doyle closes in on Malcolm MacDonald.

The game was only in the first minute of the second half when Willie Donachie sent the ball toward Newcastle's far post where Tommy Booth was on hand to head it across the goal area. Denis Tueart, with his back to the goal, then performed an overhead kick worthy of the great Pele. The ball bounced by Newcastle keeper Mike Mahoney and into the bottom left of the net to make it 2-1 to City. This was the final score though Joe Royle had a goal disallowed. City's win meant Tony Book became the first person to win the League Cup both as a player and a manager.

Ooooo! That could spoil your whole day. Ipswich Town's George Burley kicks through the legs of Brian Kidd in this near top-of-the-table clash at Maine Road on 2 April 1977. The race for the First Division title was on and both City and Ipswich were contenders. Brian Kidd opened the scoring with a 45th minute goal, with Trevor Whymark snatching the equaliser in the 90th minute. However, the smiles were soon wiped off the Tractor Boys' faces when, less than a minute later, Dave Watson scored for City. In the end Liverpool took the title with 57points. City and Ipswich tied on 56points, goal difference putting City in the runners-up place. Signed for City from United for £100,000 in 1976, Brian Kidd had three seasons at Maine Road, playing 127 full matches and scoring 57 goals. In March 1979 he was signed by Everton for £150,000.

(Below). Mike Channon joined City from Southampton in July 1977 for what was then a Maine Road record fee of £300,000. The previous record was the £275,000 plus £75,000 paid to Sunderland in March 1974 for Dennis Tueart and Mick Horswill.

Manchester United FC

Matt Busby retired as first team manager in June 1969 to become the club's general manager. His successor, Wilf McGuinness, had joined United as a player in 1953, making his senior team debut on 8 October 1955 against Wolverhampton Wanderers. However, a broken leg during the 1959-60 season cut short his playing career. Wilf moved over to the coaching staff and in 1964 was appointed reserve team manager. At the time, United's first team was still in a state of transition and major honours eluded them, though they did win the third-place play-off against Watford in the 1970 FA Cup competition.

With the first team still short of one or two key players, the 1970-71 campaign did not get off to a flying start. The opening game on 15 August saw 59,523 fans make their way to Old Trafford to watch the Reds take on Leeds United - 1968 League Cup Winners, 1968 Fairs Cup Winners, 1969 Division One Champions and 1970 runners-up in both Division One and the FA Cup. The matched ended 0-1 to Leeds. Four days later, United drew 0-0 at home against Chelsea. On 22 August, they played Arsenal at Highbury. The Gunners were always difficult to beat on their home turf and this game proved to be no different as they thrashed United 4-0.

(Middle and bottom left). Introduced in 1970, the Watney-Mann Invitation Cup was a short-lived pre-season tournament involving the previous season's two highest scoring clubs from each of the four divisions. Clubs taking part in 1970 were Manchester United and Derby County from the First Division, Hull City and Sheffield United from the Second, Fulham and Reading from the Third and Aldershot and Peterborough United from the Fourth. It was a straight knockout competition with no replays – drawn games were decided on penalty shootouts. These images are from the final between United and Derby County at the Baseball Ground on 8 August 1970. Derby County won 4-1 and Roy MacFarland is pictured here scoring the Rams' first. In the other picture Bobby Charlton looks somewhat dejected as the Rams celebrate. United competed in the 1971 Watney Cup but were knocked out in the First Round by Halifax Town of the Third Division.

UNITED REVIEW
1/-
5NP
THE OFFICIAL PROGRAMME OF MANCHESTER UNITED FOOTBALL CLUB LTD
MANCHESTER UNITED FOOTBALL CLUB
MANCHESTER UNITED
VERSUS
MANCHESTER CITY
DECEMBER 12th 1970 · KICK-OFF 2.30 pm No 15

SONS LTD
RIZLA
HACIEN

(Opposite page, top right). Between 3 and 19 April 1971, United played no less than six games. On 3 April, they lost 2-1 at West Ham. A week later the Reds entertained Derby County at Old Trafford and 45,691 fans turned up to watch the Rams – often a bit wobbly away from home – surprisingly take the points by winning 1-2. Our image was taken on 12 April and United were again at home, this time facing Wolverhampton Wanderers. Here, Wolves centre-back Frank Munro and United's George Best go for the ball. If United were hoping to put the Rams tie behind them, they were in luck as a goal by Alan Gowling in the 45th minute was enough.

(Opposite page bottom). John Aston beats Southampton's Joe Kirkup to the ball during the First Division game at the Dell on Saturday 21 November 1970. From the opening game of the season against Leeds to the thrilling 4-4 Boxing Day draw at Derby County, United had played twenty-three First Division games. They had won just five – against Burnley, Everton, Coventry City, West Bromwich Albion and Nottingham Forest. Of the remainder, nine games had ended in draws and nine were lost. On 29 December, Wilf McGuinness was sacked; Matt Busby taking charge until the end of the season.

(Above). Alex Stepney saves from the feet of Wolves' midfielder Jim McCalliog. McCalliog signed for Wolves in 1969 and made 163 appearances for them before moving to Old Trafford in 1974. His stay was short, moving to Southampton in 1975 after making 31 appearances for the Red Devils. The day after this game, United were away to Coventry City and again lost 2-1. On 17 April, United were at Crystal Palace, winning 3-5 thanks to a hat-trick from Denis Law and two from George Best. On 19 April, United faced Liverpool at Anfield and again lost 2-0. United finished the season in eighth place.

Due to a knife-throwing incident at a match at the end of the previous season, the FA ordered United to play their first two home ties of the 1971-72 season at neutral grounds. On 20 August, United faced Arsenal at Anfield, winning 3-1 with goals from Bobby Charlton, Alan Gowling and Brian Kidd. On 23 August, United clashed with West Bromwich Albion at Stoke City's Victoria Ground, where again they won 3-1 thanks to two from George Best and one from Alan Gowling. These images, taken at Anfield, show that the crowd problems had not gone away.

It was Frank O'Farrell's first season in charge and by Christmas United were top of the league. Then it all went horribly wrong with a run of seven defeats in a row, including three at home against Wolves, Chelsea and Newcastle United and an away 5-1 hammering by Leeds United at Elland Road. United had little luck in domestic cup competitions either. In the Third Round of the FA Cup, it took a replay to dispose of Southampton, though the Fourth Round was a straight 2-0 win over Preston North End. Again, in the Fifth Round, it took a replay for United to overcome Middlesbrough, though the end of the road came in the Sixth. It was yet another replay but this time it was Stoke City who emerged the victors. Stoke City proved to be United's nemesis in the Fourth Round of the League Cup. The met at Old Trafford on 27 October 1971, the game ending 1-1. The replay at the Victoria Ground on 8 November ended in a goalless draw. The second replay on 15 November ended 2-1 to Stoke City.

The run of seven league defeats in a row forced O'Farrell to strengthen United's defence by signing Martin Buchan from Aberdeen for £125,000. United finished the season in eighth place.

A former Old Trafford great returns. The one and only Collyhurst-born Nobby Stiles - toothless, short-sighted, but still an outstanding tough-tackling, ball-winning, defensive midfielder. Nobby joined United on schoolboy forms in 1957, turning professional two years later and making his League debut against Bolton Wanderers in 1960. He made a total of 363 appearances for United and was capped 28 times by England. His aggressive no-nonsense style in the 1966 World Cup resulted in Eusebio being effectively marked out of the game during England's semi-final against Portugal. In 1971, Nobby was transferred to Middlesbrough for £20,000. He made 57 appearances for the north-east club before being released in August 1973, whereupon he joined up with Bobby Charlton at Preston North End. He played 46 times for Preston, becoming their manager in 1977. Our image, taken on 26 February 1972, shows Nobby walking out on to the Old Trafford pitch for Middlesbrough's FA Cup Fifth Round tie against United. It ended 0-0, though United won the replay 0-3 with goals from Willie Morgan, George Best and Bobby Charlton.

Saturday 27 April 1974 and United have it all to play for. Their opponents were none other than City and at stake was United's survival in the First Division. To avoid relegation, United had to win and both West Ham United and Birmingham City had to lose. With just eight minutes left, Denis Law backheeled the ball past Alex Stepney to score the only goal of the game. Here, *MEN* photographer John Fowler captures the immediate aftermath. There is no celebration from the former Old Trafford idol as an ashen-faced Denis Law realises he has hammered a nail in the coffin of his former team-mates. The image below shows the reaction as hundreds of United fans invaded the pitch. Referee David Smith had no alternative and abandoned the match. If United fans thought their invasion would help the club, they were wrong. Both the Hammers and Birmingham won their games and, on 3 May, the League announced that the Old Trafford result would stand.

It was United's first season in the Second Division since 1937-38 and it opened on 17 August with an away fixture against Orient, where both points were secured thanks to goals from Willie Morgan and left-back Stewart Houston. The top two images on this page were taken the following Saturday as United fans made their way to Old Trafford for the first home game of the season against Millwall. 44,756 fans turned up to watch United tear the Londoners apart 4-0. Gerry Daly scored three – including two penalties – and Stuart Pearson netted the other.

On 28 August, United's third fixture of the season was a home tie against Portsmouth. Once again, United took both points thanks to Gerry Daly scoring from the penalty spot and a goal from Sammy McIlroy. By 28 September, when United travelled to Carrow Road to face Norwich City, they had played nine League games, winning seven and drawing two. Interestingly, Norwich had also been relegated at the end of the previous season and, under their manager John Bond, were looking for a quick return to top flight football. The game went Norwich's way by two goals to nil.

On 15 March 1975, Norwich came to Old Trafford for the return fixture and managed to leave with a point following the 1-1 draw. Norwich turned out to be United's League Cup nemesis when they clashed in the semi-finals. The first leg at Old Trafford had finished 2-2 with Lou Macari netting both of United's goals. The second leg at Carrow Road ended 1-0 to Norwich.

In the FA Cup, United made a shock exit in the Third Round to lowly Walsall. The Third Division side came to Old Trafford with few expectations other than enjoying their football. However, they held the Red Devils to a goalless draw and then won the replay 3-2 after extra time.

At the end of the season, both United and Norwich City were promoted back to the First Division.

(Bottom). Stretford-Enders caged into the terraces. The image is thought to date from August 1974.

(Left). Manchester United's old boys returned to Old Trafford on 26 November 1975 to play in Pat Crerand's testimonial against the then current side. Back row, left to right: David Herd, David Sadler, Alex Stepney, Pat Crerand, Seamus Brennan, Brian Kidd, Francis Burns and Sir Matt Busby. Front row, left to right: Bobby Charlton, Nobby Stiles, Denis Law, Tony Dunne and George Best.

(Middle). 1976 FA Cup semi-final against Derby County at Hillsborough. Steve Coppell is challenged by Derby's left back David Nish. United went through to the final thanks to two goals from Gordon Hill. The other semi-final played that day was between Crystal Palace of the Third Division and Second Division Southampton. Goals from Andy Gilchrist and David Peach (penalty) would put the Saints through to the final.

The League title was still up for grabs and within the reach of six clubs – including United. On Easter Saturday, Liverpool went top following a 5-3 win a Stoke City. QPR lost at Norwich, whilst the current champions, Derby County, blew it by drawing at home against Leicester City. Two days later, Liverpool beat Manchester City 3-0, QPR bounced Arsenal 2-1 and a goal from Lou Macari was enough to relegate Burnley. United were tantalisingly close to pulling off a double when, on 21 April, they played mid-table Stoke City at Old Trafford in front of 53,879 fans – about 8000 fewer than had turned up to Old Trafford on 17 April to see the Red Devils beat Everton 2-1. The Stoke game did not go well. United lost 0-1, leaving them anchored in third place, the title out of reach. On 24 April – the last Saturday of the season - QPR went top with a 2-0 win over Leeds United, though they knew Liverpool could overtake them to win the title by one point. Liverpool did just that.

Fans on their way to the 1976 FA Cup Final against Southampton.

MANCHESTER UNITED
O.P.E REDS
WAY OUT
WAY OUT
COZ THE
UNITED

On 1 May 1976, United's FA Cup hopes were running high. They had finished in third place in the League, just four points adrift of champions Liverpool. Southampton had finished the season in sixth place in the Second Division, seven points behind Sunderland. On paper, it ought to have been United's final.

In the first fifteen minutes Southampton's keeper Ian Turner saved from Gerry Daly and Gordon Hill and Southampton's defence and midfield worked tirelessly to break up numerous United raids. Despite this, the match was not one-sided and Mike Channon came close on a couple of occasions only to be thwarted by Alex Stepney.

Stuart Pearson gets his legs removed from under him.

Steve Coppell is almost surrounded by Saints' players including Mick Channon and Nick Holmes. In the 83rd minute, Saints' midfielder Jim McCalliog hit a pass to Bobby Stokes who slammed it into the far corner, putting the Hampshire side ahead. There were appeals for offside. Referee Clive Thomas checked with his linesmen and awarded the goal.

(Opposite page, top). United fans at Wembley 1976.

(Opposite page, bottom). Steve Coppell is chased by Saints' defender David Peach.

FOOTBALL ASSOCIATION
CHALLENGE CUP COMPETITION
FINAL
Liverpool
Manchester
United
SATURDAY
21st MAY
1977
Kick off 3pm
WEMBLEY STADIUM
Silver Jubilee Year Official Cup Final Programme 50p

WAY OUT
RIZLA

(Above). Alex Stepney jumps to clear away a Liverpool attack.

(Opposite page, top right). Arthur Albiston gets the better of Liverpool skipper Emlyn Hughes and makes off with the ball during the 1977 FA Cup Final. Stuart Pearson put United ahead in the 51st minute when he rammed home past Liverpool keeper Ray Clemence. The celebrations were short-lived, for just two minutes later Jimmy Case made it 1-1 when he hooked a half-volley clear of Alex Stepney.

(Opposite page, bottom). The smiles were soon wiped off Liverpool's faces when, in the 55th minute, Jimmy Greenhoff got in the way of Lou Macari's shot and the ball was deflected into the net to make it 2-1.

(Right). Following United's defeat in the 1976 Final, 'The Doc' promised the team would bounce back and win the trophy. To prove it, here he is holding the 1977 FA Cup aloft. Docherty could do no wrong: that is until his affair with the wife of club physiotherapist Laurie Brown became public. The tabloid press had a field day. On 4 July 1977, Docherty was sacked after 215 games in charge at Old Trafford.

To reach the 1979 FA Cup Final, United had beaten Chelsea, Fulham, Colchester United, Tottenham Hotspur, and Liverpool. Of these, the games against Fulham, Spurs and Liverpool had gone to replays. The Final was against Arsenal, who had finished the season in seventh place in the First Division on 48points – two places and three points above United.

It was the Gunners who opened the scoring in the 12th minute. The move started with Liam Brady who made a long pass to Frank Stapleton. He passed the ball to David Price who then centred it into United's goalmouth where Brian Talbot was waiting to put it into the back of the net. For the next half hour, United dominated the play. In the 43rd minute a cross from Liam Brady found Frank Stapleton, who headed it in. The second half flowed but it looked as if Arsenal were going to take home the silverware. Then, in the 86th minute, Gordon McQueen pulled one back for United. Two minutes later, Sammy McIlroy levelled when he dribbled round two Arsenal defenders.

Goal scorer Sammy McIlroy is congratulated by Martin Buchan.

It looked as if the game would go into extra time. United were still congratulating themselves when Liam Brady made a long diagonal run and kicked the ball out to Graham Rix on the left of the park. He, in turn, placed a curving centre to the far post for Alan Sunderland to hit home in the 89th minute. Martin Buchan looks on as Arsenal's Alan Sunderland celebrates and Frank Stapleton rushes in to congratulate him. Team-mate Brian Talbot (right) does his own thing. Little wonder this match became known as the 'Five-minute Final.'

Oldham Athletic FC

Swansea City winger Brian Evans puts the ball out of reach of Latics' keeper Barry Gordine to score the first of Swansea's four goals on 7 February 1970. This away defeat left Oldham firmly anchored in 22nd position in the Fourth Division, whilst Swansea jumped ahead of Brentford and Wrexham into second place behind eventual division title-winners Chesterfield. The season ended with Oldham in 19th position on 39 points. Swansea were promoted along with Wrexham, Port Vale and title winners Chesterfield. If Oldham had had a narrow escape, spare a thought for poor old Bradford Park Avenue – once a First Division side and FA Cup quarterfinalists in 1913, 1920 and 1946. They had finished bottom of the Fourth Division in 1967-68, 1968-69 and now again in 1969-70, forcing them to seek re-election. It should have been a foregone conclusion – after all Port Vale had automatically been re-elected at the end of the 1967-68 season despite being kicked out for making unauthorised payments. But the times they were a changing and Bradford PA were booted out in favour of Cambridge United. For those of you interested in former Oldham players, Barry Gordine joined the Latics from Sheffield United in 1968, making 83 senior appearances before being transferred to Southend United in 1971.

Oldham Athletic players, apprentices and coaching staff pose for the camera. Back row, left to right: Derek Spencer, Chris Ogden, Ian Taylor and Keith Hicks. Middle row standing, left to right: Jimmy Frizzell (manager), Ian Robins, Alan McNeill, Jim Bowie, David Shaw, Don Heath, Harry Dowd, Bill Cranston, Dick Mulvaney, Jim 'Pancho' Fryatt, Mike Lester, Walter Joyce and Jim McGregor. Seated, left to right: Steve Hoolickin, Ian Wood, Maurice Whittle, Tommy Bryceland, Keith Bebbington, Paul Clements and Kevin Devine. On the ground, left to right: Andy Sweeney, Steve Bambrough, Kevin Crumblehulme, John Duddy, Bob Sykes, Pat Phillips and Ian Buckley.

The first team pose for a group photograph. Back row, left to right: Jim Bowie, David Shaw, Chris Ogden, Don Heath, Harry Dowd, Bill Cranston and Dick Mulvaney. Front row, left to right: Alan McNeill, Ian Wood, Maurice Whittle, Tommy Bryceland, Keith Bebbington, Paul Clements and Jim 'Pancho' Fryatt.

Midfielder Jim Bowie joined the Latics from Arthurlie Juniors in July 1962, making 331 appearances, plus two more as a sub and scoring 37 goals. He transferred to Rochdale in October 1972.

David Shaw was a striker who joined Oldham from Huddersfield Town as part of an exchange deal that saw Les Chapman move to the Yorkshire side. David made 155 senior appearances for Oldham, scoring 70 goals. In March 1973, he moved to West Bromwich Albion for £80,000. In October 1975, he returned to the Latics on a free transfer and made a further 59 appearances, scoring 21 goals, before being forced to retire due to a knee injury.

Goalkeeper Chris Ogden signed from the junior side in July 1971, making 128 appearances before being transferred to Swindon Town in August 1978. Though he managed 22 appearances for them during the 1978-79 season, Chris was pretty much Swindon's second choice keeper to Jimmy Allen. After fifteen months, he moved to Rotherham United. Chris's father Fred, had also kept goal for Oldham.

A native of Stockton-On-Tees, outside-right Don Heath arrived at Oldham in July 1970 on a transfer from Swindon Town. He made 45 appearances for the Latics, scoring one goal, before moving to Peterborough United on a free transfer in July 1972. In July 1973, he signed for Hartlepool United and moved to non-league football during 1977, playing for Crook Town, Gateshead and South Bank.

Former Manchester City goalkeeper Harry Dowd joined the Latics in December 1970, making 131 senior appearances including League, FA Cup, and League Cup games. He later joined Northwich Victoria.

Centre-back Bill Cranston joined Oldham from Preston North End in July 1970, where, despite only making sixteen appearances, had been named their Player of the Year 1969-70. At Oldham Bill made 98 appearances plus two as a sub, scoring two goals.

Central defender Dick Mulvaney was signed by Blackburn Rovers in February 1964, from non-league Billingham Synthonia. He joined Oldham in August 1971, making 88 appearances, plus four as sub, scoring two goals. In October 1974, he moved to Rochdale where he made 72 appearances, plus one as a sub, scoring four goals.

Alan McNeill was a midfielder signed from Huddersfield Town in October 1969. At Oldham, he made 154 appearances, with a further sixteen as a sub, scoring nineteen goals. In July 1975, he moved to Stockport County where he made 69 appearances, plus two as a sub, scoring one goal. He later played non-league football with Witton Albion and Macclesfield Town.

Right-back Ian Wood holds the record for the number of appearances for Oldham Athletic. Ian was signed from Park Lane Olympic in November 1965 and went on to make 517 appearances, plus seven as a sub scoring 22 goals. On 27 April 1974, he fell badly and dislocated a shoulder during a game against York City. Unable to play in the next fixture (against Charlton Athletic), his run of consecutive games (161) came to an end. During the summer of 1974, he went on loan to the Denver Dynamos in the US and was loaned to the San Jose Earthquakes during 1978-79. In May 1980, he signed for Burnley and in 1981 returned to the US to play for the Wichita Wings. He ended his playing career at Radcliffe Borough.

Maurice Whittle arrived at Boundary Park in May 1969, having been signed from Blackburn Rovers. In a career spanning nearly seven years, Maurice, who played left-back, made 307 appearances, plus five as a sub, scoring 39 goals. He was another League player to go to the US, where he played 80 times for the Fort Lauderdale Strikers. In 1979, he returned to the UK and signed for Barrow, moving in March 1980 to Wigan Athletic. He later played for Barrow and Macclesfield Town.

Tommy Bryceland spent much of his career with Norwich City before signing for Oldham in March 1970. The midfielder made 66 appearances for the Latics, scoring ten goals, before returning to his first club, St Mirren, in 1971 as player-manager.

Winger Keith Bebbington was signed from Stoke City in August 1966 and for six years was a regular first-team player, notching up a grand total of 237 League appearances, scoring 39 goals. When FA Cup and League Cup appearances are taken into consideration, Keith's appearances for the Latics came to 255 and 46 goals. In July 1972, he was transferred to Rochdale where he made 57 appearances, plus three as a sub, scoring six goals.

Midfielder Paul Clements had won eight England Amateur International caps whilst playing for non-league Skelmersdale United. Signed by Oldham in June 1971, he made 32 appearances plus three as a sub for the club before returning to non-league football with Wigan Athletic and later Altrincham.

When Jim Fryatt, a stockily built centre-forward joined Oldham from Blackburn Rovers in February 1970, he had already led a somewhat nomadic footballing life, having been with Charlton Athletic, Bradford Park Avenue, Southport, Torquay United and Stockport County. He signed for Southport in November 1971, after making 76 appearances and scoring 40 goals for the Latics. Later teams included second spells at both Stockport County and Torquay United, as well as playing in the US for the Philadelphia Atoms, Hartford Bicentennials, and managing the Las Vegas Quicksilvers. Jim holds the record for the fastest goal in the Football League. On 25 April 1964, whilst playing for Bradford Park Avenue against Tranmere Rovers, he scored four seconds after the kick-off.

A string of defeats in late 1973 left Oldham stuck on 24 points in ninth position in the Third Division, thirteen points behind leaders Bristol Rovers. Then it all changed. From their 1-2 away win at Wrexham on 12 January, to their 2-1 home win over York City on 12 March, the Latics won ten games on the trot, climbing to second place.

(Right). 15,871 fans turned out at Burden Park on 12 March 1974 to watch Oldham take on York City. At the time, it was Oldham's largest gate of the season and they were not disappointed as full-back Maurice Whittle scored both Latics' goals, including a penalty, in the 2-1 victory that put them just five points behind leaders Bristol Rovers with three games in hand.

(Middle). The surprise 1-0 defeat at Chesterfield on 16 March 1974 still left Oldham in second place on goal difference from York City, though here too the Latics had games in hand. On 19 March, they played at home against Bournemouth. Two goals from Colin Garwood, and one apiece from Ronnie Blair and Ian Robins earned the points in the 4-2 win. Oldham played nine League games during March: the last three were a 1-1 draw at home against Hereford United; a 1-4 away defeat at Charlton Athletic, and a 2-0 away win at Shrewsbury Town.

Then came hectic April. The Latics defeated Grimsby Town 3-1, drew 2-2 with Tranmere Rovers, and hammered Southport 6-0. The 0-2 win at Southport on 15 April took Oldham to the top of the division, a point clear and two games in hand over Rovers, and a win against Huddersfield Town on 20 April would secure Oldham a promotion place. The 'War of the Roses' tie at Boundary Park culminated in the Yorkshire side being torn apart 6-0. Our image features Latics' manager Jimmy Frizzell acknowledging a sea of fans after the club had clinched one of the three promotion places with 60 points. Of their three remaining fixtures, Oldham drew 1-1 with York City, lost 0-2 at home to Charlton Athletic and drew 0-0 at Plymouth Argyle to finish on 62 points and take the Third Division title. Bristol Rovers and York City both finished the season on 61 points.

For the 1973-74 season, the Football League had modified promotion and relegation between the divisions. It would be three down from the First; three up, three down from the Second; three up, four down from the Third, and four up from the Fourth. Southampton, Manchester United and Norwich City were relegated from the First. Middlesbrough, Luton Town and Carlisle United were promoted to the First and Crystal Palace, Preston North End and Swindon Town relegated to the Third. Oldham Athletic, Bristol Rovers and York City were promoted to the Second, whilst Cambridge United, Shrewsbury Town, Southport United and Rochdale were banished to the Fourth. Peterborough United, Gillingham, Colchester United and Bury were promoted to the Third. Once again Stockport County were forced to seek re-election.

(Bottom). Oldham's John Platt and Bolton Wanderers' full-back Peter Nicholson holding hands as they tangle for the ball. The Second Division clash, on 23 October 1976, ended 2-2. Oldham finished the season in thirteenth position on 38 points, Bolton in fourth on 51 points

Oldham Athletic were having a good season when they travelled to Craven Cottage for their Second Division game against Fulham on 4 December 1976. The Latics were in sixth position, seven places ahead of Fulham. Both sides had good home records but were equally as flaky when playing away, but the advantage was with Fulham. The game attracted a larger-than-usual gate as the Manchester United v QPR game had been postponed and United fans turned up to watch their former idol, George Best, play for Fulham. Oldham, playing in their strip of tangerine shirts, white shorts and tangerine socks kicked-off, but it wasn't long before keeper John Platt made a brilliant save from Fulham's John Mitchell. At half-time, Fulham were 1-0 ahead thanks to a header from John Mitchell. In the second-half Teddy Maybank – who was on loan from Chelsea – scored Fulham's second following a free kick awarded for a foul on George Best. Maybank also scored Fulham's third and George Best got the fourth when he noticed John Platt was off his line and chipped the ball off the crossbar and into the back of the net. John Mitchell made it 5-0 when he turned in a cross from Les Barrett. Despite the setback, Oldham finished the season in thirteenth position on 38 points; Fulham finished seventeenth on 35 points. In our image, Oldham's David Shaw (No.8) is unable to stop George Best.

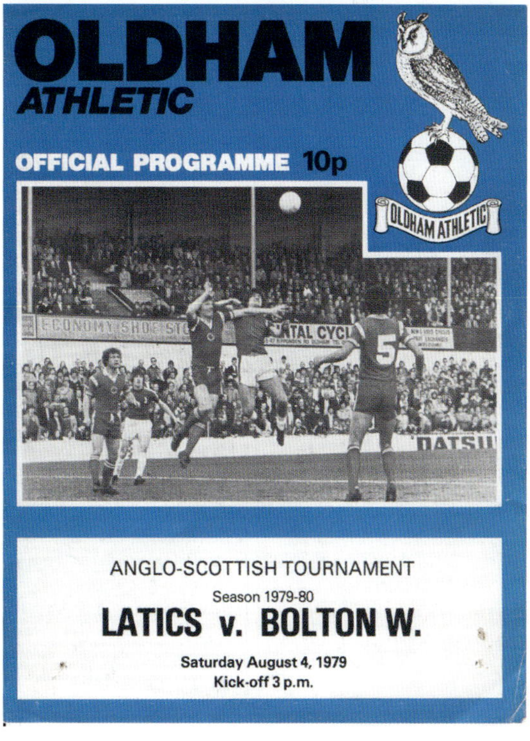

Rochdale FC

Rochdale v Coventry City, January 1971. Cross scores for Rochdale.

Swansea City v Rochdale, 30 October 1971. The ball is a blur as Rochdale keeper Tony Godfrey does his best to block it. Swansea won 1-0.

Rochdale pose for the camera prior to the start of the 1977-78 season. Back row, left to right: Billy Boslem, Bobby Scott, Chris Shyne, Bob Mountford, Ian Bannon and Nigel O'Loughlan. Front row, left to right: Dave Esser, Ian Seddon, Steve Melledew, Paul Hallows and Alan Tarbuck. Sitting: Steve Shaw and Ted Oliver.

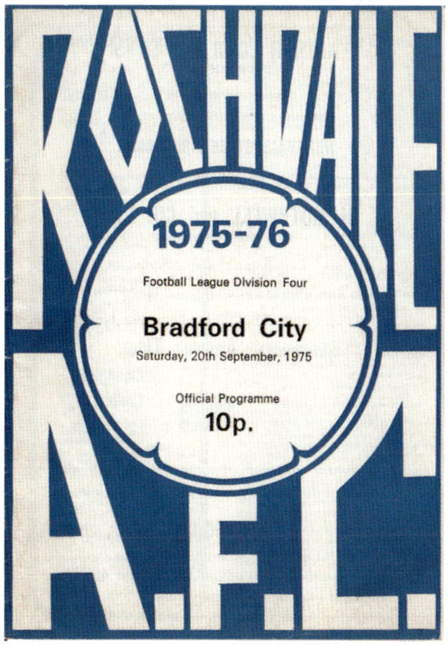

At the end of the 1968-69 season, Rochdale, the 1962 League Cup runners-up, were promoted for the first time in their history. The club was on a roll during the 1970-71 season, winning the Lancashire Cup – their previous success being the 1948-49 competition and proceeding as far as the Fourth Round of the FA Cup before being hammered 5-0 by Fourth Division Colchester in a replay. But life in the Third Division would be short-lived. The 1973-74 season was dire. The club finished bottom of the Division, winning just two of their 46 League fixtures, though they did draw seventeen others, giving them a grand total of 21points and an appalling goal difference of 38 for and 94 against. Little did they know at the time, but they were about to set a unique Football League record of remaining for 36 consecutive seasons in the bottom division.

It could have been worse. At the end of the 1977-78 season, they were bottom of the Division on 24 points and forced to seek re-election. They must have had friends in high places as Southport, who had finished one place above them, were kicked out of the League and replaced by Wigan Athletic. It was a close-run thing at the end of the 1979-80 season when once again the club sought re-election. They made it by just one vote over Altrincham.

Grandstand?

Lancashire CCC

It was an interesting time to follow Lancashire County Cricket Club. Introduced in 1963, the Gillette Cup was the first top-level, single-innings, one-day limited-over knock-out competition for English and Welsh county sides. Sides were limited to a maximum of 65 overs and, as each bowler could bowl a maximum of fifteen overs, sides had to field at least five bowlers. Lancashire's claim to fame in the first Gillette Cup competition is that they took part in the very first match to be played when they faced Leicestershire at Old Trafford on 1 May 1963. The following year, the number of overs was reduced to 60, the maximum for each bowler reduced to thirteen overs per match and teams from the Minor Counties were allowed to compete for the first time.

Fast forward to the beginning of the Seventies. The final, at Lord's, of the 1970 Gillette Cup saw Lancashire pitted against Sussex, winners in 1963 and 1964, and runners-up to Warwickshire in 1968. Lancs made 185 for four (55.1 overs), Sussex reached 184 for nine, giving Lancashire a six-wicket victory. The following year, Lancs were again in the final, this time the opposition was Kent, winners in 1967. After 60 overs, Lancs were 224 for seven and in reply Kent were all out for 200 (56.2 overs), giving Lancashire a win by 24 runs. Lancashire returned to Lord's in 1972 for an unprecedented third final in a row, facing Warwickshire, winners of the 1966 and 1968 finals and runners-up in 1964. After 56.4 overs, Lancs were on 235 for six. Warwickshire made 234 for nine, giving Lancashire a win by four wickets.

Though the 1973 final was played between Gloucestershire and Sussex, Lancashire were not a spent force as 1974 saw them back facing old foes Kent. However, the dream of four Gillette Cups in five years was short-lived as Kent won by four wickets. The dream of four Gillette Cups in six years turned into reality as their 1975 opponents Middlesex made 180 for eight (60 overs) to Lancashire's 182 for 3 (57 overs).

1976 saw Lancashire in the Gillette final for the sixth time in seven years. That year's competition had been played by seventeen first-class sides and the Minor Counties sides Berkshire, Hertfordshire, Lincolnshire, Shropshire and Staffordshire. Lancashire entered the competition in the second round when they faced Middlesex at Old Trafford on 14 July. Middlesex were 270 for nine after 60 overs, bowler Allan Jones having taken three of their wickets for 52 runs. Lancs reached 271 in 58.4 overs with Harry Pilling making 82 runs. Harry was player of the match.

The quarter final against 1973 Gillette winners Gloucestershire was played at Old Trafford on 4 August. The visitors were all out for 125 (57.1 overs), Jack Davey taking two for six runs. Going in to bat, Lancashire took just 37.2 overs to hit 128 having lost three wickets. Barry Wood, who made 62, was made player of the match.

The semi-final was played against Warwickshire at Edgbaston on 18 August. The home side were all out for 233, Steve Rouse taking two for 41 in twelve overs. Lancs went through to the final, hitting 234 for four with Barry Wood making a respectable 104. Once again Barry Wood was made player of the match.

As always, the Gillette final was at Lord's. It was Lancashire's sixth final in seven years and Northamptonshire's first. After 60 overs, Lancashire were on 195 for seven with David Lloyd hitting 48 runs. Northamptonshire went in to bat and despite bowler Bishan Bedi taking three wickets for 52 runs in eleven overs, they hung on reaching 199 for six after 58.1 overs. It was Lancashire's last appearance in a Gillette Cup final, though they would return in 1986, by which time the competition had been renamed the NatWest Trophy.

Lancashire CCC player David Lloyd tries out a head guard manufactured by Cooper Cricket. Protective headwear for batsmen had its origins back in the 1930s, but changes in fast bowling during the late-1960s led to fresh calls for protective headgear for batsmen. Sunil Gavaskar, opening batsman for India adopted a skull cap that owed more to rugby league than the motorcycle-helmet style taken up by England players Tony Greig and Dennis Amiss.

Lancashire v Glamorgan in the John Player League at Old Trafford on 12 September 1971. Matches were played on Sundays and limited to 40 overs per side. In this match, Glamorgan were 143 all out (37.4 overs) and Lancashire were 109 all out (34.3 overs). Worcestershire won the title. Lancashire finished third and Glamorgan tenth. David Hughes had Lancashire's best bowling average: 636 balls, 24 wickets, average 15.58.

Lancashire's new captain David Lloyd leads pace bowlers Peter Lever and Ken Shuttleworth at leap-frogging during a pre-season training session at Old Trafford, April 1973. David Lloyd's first-class cricket debut for Lancashire came in June 1965 against Middlesex. A left-handed batsman and left-arm spinner, he made 19,269 runs in first-class cricket and 552 runs in Test matches. His highest score was 214 not out. David captained Lancashire 1973-77.

Press day for Lancashire CCC at Old Trafford, April 1975.

All quiet in the England dressing room on the first day of the First Test for the Ashes against Australia at Old Trafford, June 1972. England won the Toss and chose to bat. Making their test debuts were Tony Greig for England and David Colley and Bruce Francis for Australia.

Spectators bring out their brollies as play is delayed due to rain.

Aussie spinner John Gleeson appeals for lbw against England opener Geoff Boycott. England were all out for 249 (120.4 overs) in their 1st Innings. John Edrich made 49 before he was run out and newcomer Tony Greig was the side's highest scorer, making 57 runs before being given lbw, bowled David Colley. Australia's 1st Innings ended all out for 142 (58 overs). England's 2nd Innings ended all out for 234 (82.6 overs). Opener Geoff Boycott had scored 47 runs before being given out lbw, bowled John Gleeson. Once again, newcomer Tony Greig was the highest scorer with 62 runs before being bowled out be Greg Chappell.

ustralia's 2nd Innings began on the fourth day, their target 342 runs. At close of play they were 57 for two, leaving a target of 85 runs for the fifth and last day. Here, Dennis Lillie and John Gleeson, the last Aussies standing, are clapped off the field having elped their side reach a respectable 252 (85.2 overs). Leading 2nd Innings scorers were Keith Stackpole, who reached 67 before eing bowled by Tony Greig, and Rod Marsh who had racked up 91 when he was caught by wicket keeper Alan Knott.

On Saturday 31 May 1975, it had been sunshine, sunhats, shirt-sleeves, sunburn and ice-cream as Derbyshire entertained Lancashire at the Park Road Ground, Buxton. Lancashire ended their 1st Innings, declaring at 477 for five after 100 overs, with Clive Lloyd scoring 167 and Frank Hayes 104. At close of play, Derbyshire were on 25 for two. The teams did not play on Sunday, the match resuming on Monday 2 June. Well, that is what should have happened but shortly after the teams arrived in Buxton it started raining. After the rain came hail and then snow. Umpire Dickie Bird said, "When I went out to inspect the wicket, the snow was level with the top of my boots. I'd never seen anything like it". Play was cancelled for the day, resuming on Tuesday 3 June. Derbyshire were all out for 42 and forced to follow-on. The 2nd Innings proved little better. On a rock-hard wicket Derbyshire were dismissed in less than one hour for 87. It was Derbyshire's heaviest defeat of the twentieth century – an innings and 348 runs.

One of the great West Indies fast bowlers of the 1970s, Andy Roberts, does his stuff during the Third Test against England at Old Trafford in July 1976. The Pakistan captain Imran Khan reckoned Andy Roberts was one of the fastest bowlers he ever faced in a Test. Andy was the first Antiguan to play Test cricket for the West Indies.

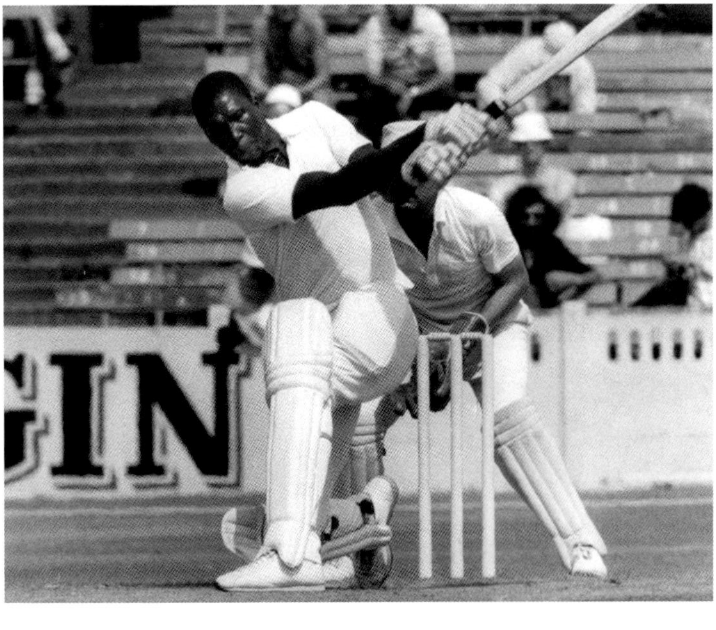

Lancs v Somerset at Old Trafford, August 1979. Somerset's West Indies, 6ft 8in (2.03metres) tall fast bowler, Joel 'Big Bird' Garner takes his turn with the bat. With this stroke Joel hit the ball out of the ground. In the 1979 Cricket World Cup Final between the West Indies and England, Joel took five wickets for 39 runs, though at one point it had been five wickets for four runs. Fast bowlers Joel Garner, Andy Roberts, Colin Croft and Michael Holden contributed to making the West Indies one of the great Test sides of the 1970s and 80s.

Little Gary Ashcroft, Leigh team mascot, waits impatiently in the team line up to meet the guests of honour alongside his father Kevin Ashcroft before the start of the 70th Rugby League Challenge Cup, against Leeds at Wembley, on 15 May 1971. Ashcroft played hooker in a game that would enter the history books for probably the wrong reason. As for Kevin Ashcroft, he moved to Warrington later in 1971 and played prop in their 24-9 victory over Featherstone Rovers in the 1974 Challenge Cup and hooker in the 14-7 defeat by Widnes in the 1975 final. He also played prop in Warrington's 0-0 draw against Salford in the 1974 BBC2 Floodlit Trophy and in the 5-10 replay defeat. He captained Warrington in their 27-16 win over Rochdale Hornets in the 1973-74 Players No6 Trophy Final.

Leeds attempt to close-down a Leigh attack. Jim Fiddler made it 0-2 to Leigh with a drop goal after just five minutes which was interesting as, from the start of the of the 1971-72 season, a drop goal would earn only one point. Skipper Alex 'Yapper' Murphy (almost hidden by a Leeds player) appears to be having his legs removed from under him, though Pete Smethurst (No.13) is coming round to support.

(Top). Stuart Ferguson (No.2) jumps as Stan Dorrington's (No.3) scores a try following a scrum close to Leeds' try line. Alex Murphy (No.7) almost made it to the line himself but managed to pass the ball to Stan who grounded it, making it 0-7. Stan Ferguson converted bringing the tally to 0-9. Stan's try was the first Leeds had conceded in the whole competition.

(Right). Pete Smethurst (No.13) and Geoff Clarkson (No.12) move in to close down a rare Leeds attack the Leigh try line.

The referee Billy Thompson intervenes as players square up to one another. There were a few blow-ups after hard tackles. The most famous incident of the match occurred during the second half between Leigh's Alex 'Yapper' Murphy and Leeds' Syd Hynes. It ended when Hynes headbutted Yapper. Yapper was stretchered off and Syd, after Billy Thompson had conferred with touch judge Tom Crowley, was sent off and in doing so became the first player ever to have been given his marching orders during a Challenge Cup final.

Leeds' skipper Syd Hynes heads for the early bath after being sent off. Syd always maintained he never touched Yapper. "No. Never made contact", he said. "If I'd made contact he'd wouldn't have got off that stretcher winkin' to all the crowd".

Leigh celebrate their 24-7 victory over Leeds. It was Leigh's first appearance in a Challenge Cup final since their 13-0 win over Halifax in 1921.

Images from the 1971-72 Challenge Cup Quarter Final match between Salford and Wigan. It ended 21-9 to Salford, who went on to meet, and lose against, Leeds in the semi-finals. Salford and Wigan were evenly matched in that season's Championship. Both had played 34 matches, both had won 25, both had drawn none, both had lost nine and both were on 50points. The title went to Leeds on 58points: Bradford Northern were runners-up on 54points and St Helen's third on 53points.

Part of the huge crowd that turned up at Wilderspool in February 1973 to watch Warrington take on Widnes. Warrington went on to win the Championship with 56points, St Helens were fourth with 50points, Salford were sixth on 50points, Oldham ninth on 42points, Rochdale Hornets eleventh on 41points, Widnes twelfth on 38points, Leigh thirteenth on 38points and Wigan sixteenth on 35points. Salford beat Swinton 25-11 in the Lancashire County Cup, Widnes were beaten 5-0 by Leeds in the BBC2 Floodlit Trophy Final, and Widnes, who were celebrating their centenary year, played a special fixture against an 'Australians' side.

Warrington skipper Alex Murphy celebrates scoring a try in the 1974 Rugby League Challenge Cup Final. To get to the final, Warrington had disposed of Huddersfield, Huyton, Wigan and Dewsbury. Featherstone had seen off Barrow, Hull KR, Bradford Northern and Leigh.

The 1974 Rugby League Challenge Cup Final at Wembley between Warrington and Featherstone Rovers. Our image shows Warrington's Derek Whitehead kicking for goal. He scored seven goals during the match including one from the half-way line. He was awarded the Lance Todd Trophy as man of the match.

Fighting breaks out towards the end of the 1974 Rugby League Challenge Cup Final between Warrington and Featherstone Rovers. Over on the left it's a punch-up between subs as Warrington's Billy Pickup (No.14) and Featherstone's Charlie Stone (No.15) get to it. Over on the right, Mike Nicholas (No.11) is about to be set upon, though help is at hand just off camera as Dave Chisnell (No.8) and Kevin Ashcroft (No.9) were coming to the rescue when this photograph was taken. Referee Shepherd restored order and there was time enough for Alex Murphy to add another drop goal and Mike Nicholas a try, bringing the final score to 24-9 to Warrington.

Warrington's Bobby Wanbon clings to the ball despite the attention of three Featherstone Rovers players. Wanbon made 185 appearances for Warrington. A dual-code international, he won caps for Wales (RL) whilst with the club.

Warrington completing a victory lap with the Challenge Cup. Left to right: Mike Nicholas, Bobby Wanbon, Derek Noonan, Mike Philbin and Alan Whittle.

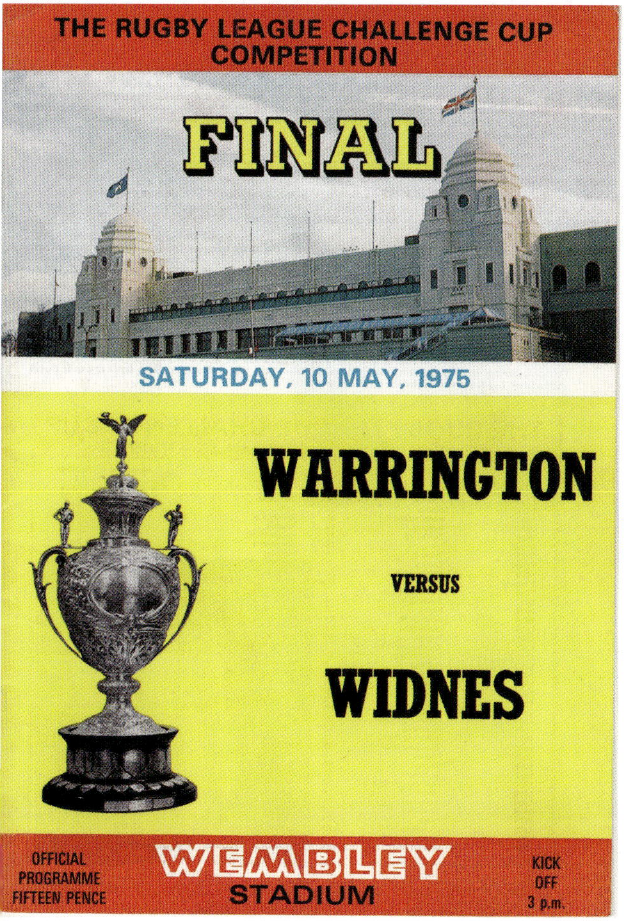

Widnes Rugby League side 1974-75 season. Back row left to right: Mick George, Mal Aspey, Ray Dutton, Jim Mills, John Foran, Mick Adams, Nick Nelson and John Wood. Front row left to right: Eric Hughes, Alan Prescott, Keith Elwell, Doug Laughton, Reg Bowden, Tony Karalius and Jim O'Neill. In a career at Widnes lasting 1966-78, Ray Dutton notched up two club records; most career goals (1083) and most career points (2195). Keith Elwell holds the record for most club appearances 587+4 between 1970-86 and Mal Aspey holds the club career try record of 234 between 1964-80.

(Left). Action from the 1975 Rugby League Challenge Cup Final.

(Middle left). Widnes scrum-half Reg Bowden (No.7) is poised to pounce. He played for Widnes in no less than sixteen cup finals, including four at Wembley. He moved to Fulham for £25,000 in 1980.

(Below). Widnes celebrate their 14-7 victory over Warrington. Widnes had been in six finals – this was their fourth win. Ray Dutton – who won the Lance Todd Trophy - had kicked five goals and a drop goal and Jim Mills had scored a try. For Warrington, Derek Whitehead had scored two goals and John Bevan a try.

(Left). Leeds are on the way to their tenth Rugby League Challenge Cup Final win as Kevin Dick scores a try against Widnes on 7 May 1977. He also scored three goals and a drop goal. Teammates Kevin Dick and Les Dyl scored a try apiece. For Widnes, Ray Dutton scored two goals and Mal Aspey a try. Leeds won 16-7. The attendance was 80,871. Throughout the decade, Lancashire was represented in all but one Challenge Cup Final. In 1970, it was Castleford v Wigan (7-2), 1971 Leigh v Leeds (24-7), 1972 St Helens v Leeds (16-13), 1974 Warrington v Featherstone Rovers (24-9), 1975 Widnes v Warrington (14-7), 1976 St Helens v Widnes (20-5), 1977 Leeds v Widnes (16-7), 1978 Leeds v St Helens (20-5) and 1979 Widnes v Wakefield Trinity (12-3).

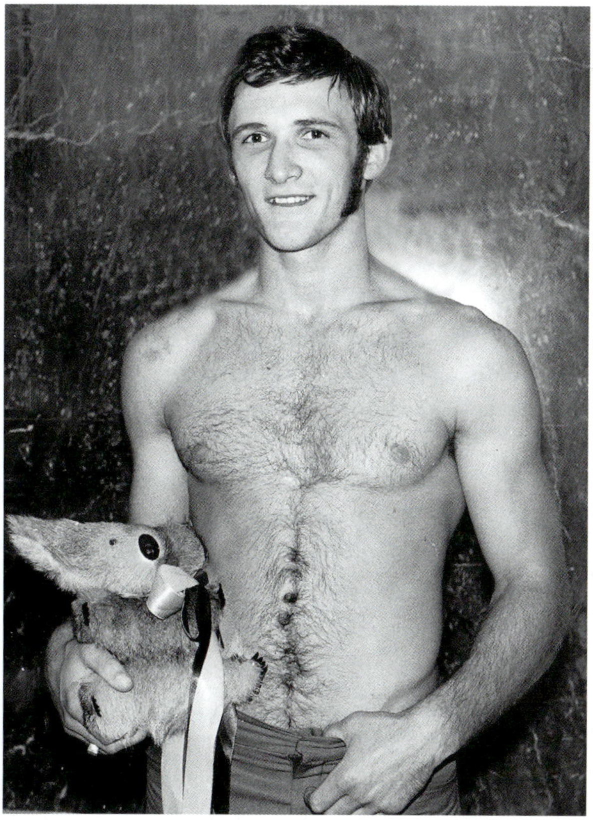

(Above right). On 20 December 1967, a young orthodox heavyweight by the name of Joe Bugner, entered the ring at the Hilton Hotel, London, for his first professional bout, only to be knocked out by his opponent, Paul Brown. Bugner then won his next eighteen bouts, including a win on points over Moses Harrell at the King's Hall, Belle Vue, on 9 June 1969. Bugner's next fight – his twentieth - was against Dick Hall at the Piccadilly Hotel, Manchester, on 5 August 1969, which he lost on points. In a career lasting 83 professional fights, his bouts against Harrell and Hall were the only two he had in Manchester.

(Above). Australian Steve Aczel fought Maxie Smith at the King's Hall, Belle Vue, on 19 February 1975 for the then vacant Commonwealth (British Empire) light heavyweight title. It was Aczel's eleventh fight as a professional and Smith's twenty-sixth. Aczel won on a technical knockout and Smith announced his retirement from the game. Four months later, Aczel defeated Tommy Mears to take the Australian light heavyweight title, though he lost both titles to Tony Mundine on 30 October 1975.

(Right). Nick Jobs putting at the 11th during the Greater Manchester Open at Wilmslow Golf Course, June 1978. Part of the European Tour Golf Tournament, the Greater Manchester Open was played annually between 1976 and 1981. It was won in 1978 by Irishman Brian Barnes, with Nick Jobs, Dennis Durnian and Bob Charles all runners-up. The last Manchester Open, held in 1981, was won by Bernard Gallacher.

Hailing from Birtle, Bury, Reg Harris was a household name in the early 1950s. In 1947, he took the amateur sprint title in the World Track Championships (WTC) as well as amateur sprint and amateur tandem sprint titles in the National Track Championships (NTC). Reg also won silver medals in both the sprint and tandem sprint (with Alan Bannister) in the 1948 Olympics, as well as taking the amateur sprint title in the NTC and coming third in the amateur sprint in the WTC. Turning professional, he took the WTC sprint titles in 1949, 1950 and 1951; came third in 1953; won the title again in 1954 and came second in 1956. Our image shows Reg at Fallowfield Racing Track in August 1971, when he might have thought his championship days were well and truly behind him. Not so, for in 1974 he again took the sprint title in the NTC. In 1950, he won the Sports Journalists Association Sportsman of the Year.

The annual Two Cities Boat Race was started by students from Manchester and Salford Universities in 1972. Our image, taken during the 1974 race, shows the teams at New Bailey bridge on the River Irwell. Manchester completed a hat-trick by beating Salford for the third time. The event was thought up and organised by the students themselves.

Punch up at Belle Vue speedway in July 1971. Belle Vue rider Alan Wilkinson and Leicester's Alan Cowland clash during a riders' free for all. July 1971.

The Belle Vue Aces make their way around the track during the team's golden jubilee celebrations in July 1978. They were following a flatbed lorry upon which were perched some of the Aces' great riders of earlier decades.

Champion trials riders Martin Lapkin (left) and Malcolm Grant (right) join road race ace Mick Grant for a speedway practice session at Belle Vue. October 1978.

Rock, Pop, Punk and Northern Soul

'Nah then, nah then, nah then, what's all this?' It's the aftermath of fans queueing for tickets for the Rolling Stones. The tarpaulins came from a building site across the street. Fans used them to keep warm as they queued overnight. Apparently, tickets were available from Manchester University students' union, where there wasn't a queue.

(Below and opposite page). Scenes from the Rolling Stones' gig at the Free Trade Hall, 5 March 1971.

wem
wem

The late 1960s were troubling times for The Bee Gees. Internal bickering culminated in March 1969 with an announcement by Robin Gibb that he was leaving the band and embarking on a solo career. Barry and Maurice Gibb went ahead, recording a new album *Cucumber Castle*, though problems remained. Drummer Colin Peterson was fired and Terry Cox from the folk-rock band Pentangle was brought in so the project could be completed. Even so, Barry and Maurice decided to go their separate ways, though the split was not announced until shortly before the album's release in May 1970. It failed to chart and though the lead-off single *Don't Forget to Remember* reached number two in the UK, it was a failure in the US where it reached number 73.

Our image, taken on 3 September 1970, shows the boys from Australia via Chorlton, back together. Barry Gibb, who just two days earlier had married beauty queen Linda Gray, had broken his honeymoon to join Robin, Maurice and new drummer Geoff Bridgford in the recording studio. In October 1970, the single *Two Years On* was released in the US and a month later in the UK. The album spawned two major singles hits in the US, though *Lonely Days* only reached number 33 in the UK. The group continued to release albums and singles with varying degrees of success but towards the end of 1974 they were in a rut, playing at small venues around the UK.

At the instigation of Robert Stigwood, the group went into the studio with R&B/soul producer Alif Mardin and recorded the album *Mr Natural.* The album also featured members of the tour band; Alan Kendall on lead guitar; Dennis Byron (ex-Amen Corner) on drums and Geoff Westley playing most of the keyboards instead of Maurice Gibb. However, Westley was soon replaced by the former Strawbs keyboard player Derek 'Blue' Weaver. Though the album failed to chart, it proved a pivotal turning point in the group's career as Stigwood and Mardin advised them to turn from ballads to more dance/disco-orientated arrangements. The band relocated to Miami where they recorded the album *Main Course*. The spin off singles *Jive Talkin'* and *Nights on Broadway* went to numbers one and seven respectively in the US. It was also their first album featuring arrangements on which Barry sang falsetto.

More hits followed and in 1975 Robert Stigwood persuaded the group to provide the soundtrack for the movie *Saturday Night Fever,* starring John Travolta. Supervised by Bill Oakes, it was at the time the world's biggest-selling soundtrack and led directly to a reinvigorated disco scene. Spin-off singles for the Bee Gees included *How Deep Is Your Love* (US number one, UK number three); *Stayin' Alive* (Number one in US and number four in the UK); *Night Fever* (number one in US and UK). More success followed. On 25 March 1978, the Bee Gees had five songs either written or recorded by themselves in the US top-ten singles charts. Their follow-up album *Spirits Having Flown* spent thirty-three weeks in the UK Charts and gave the group three more US number one singles.

It is September 1971 and Peter Noone and Herman's Hermits are at Longleat House to perform at a special birthday party for Lady Silvy Cerne Thynne, daughter of the 6th Marquess of Bath. Between August 1964 and the end of 1969, Herman's Hermits had released a string of hits on both sides of the Atlantic, with Peter Noone being the youngest vocalist to top the US singles chart. During 1970, the Hermits had chart success with the singles *Years May Come, Years May Go* (reached number 7) and *Bet Yer Life I Do* (reached number 22). By the time their third chart success of the year *Lady Barbara* (reached number 13) was released, the group had been rebranded as Peter Noone and Herman's Hermits. Less than two weeks after this photograph was taken, their album *The Most of Herman's Hermits* entered the UK album chart on a five-week run and reached number 14.

The writing was already on the wall when this photograph was taken. In May 1971, Peter Noone's solo single *Oh You Pretty Thing* entered the UK chart reaching number 12. Shortly after the Longleat gig, Noone left to pursue his solo career. The Hermits, along with new vocalist Peter Cowap, were back in Manchester in December 1971, appearing at the Odeon Cinema at a party for 3000 underprivileged children. The group signed to RCA records in the UK and recorded singles and an album at the Strawberry Studios, Stockport, where they were produced by Eric Stewart of 10cc.

Rhythm guitarist/backing vocalist Keith Hopwood left during 1972 and was replaced by John Gaugham, who in turn left in 1975 to be replaced by Frank Renshaw. Peter Noone reunited with the Hermits in 1973 for the British Invasion Tour of the US which culminated in a standing-room only show at Madison Square Garden. In 1977, K-Tel records issued a *Greatest Hits* album which reached number 37 in the UK chart.

Broughton-born Elkie Brooks performing with Vinegar Joe in 1972. The band, centred round Elkie, husband Peter Gage and Robert Palmer, released three albums: *Vinegar Joe and Rock 'n' Roll Gypsies* (both 1972) and *Six Star General* (1973). Vinegar Joe disbanded in March 1973. Elkie's first solo album *Rich Man's Woman* was well received. In 1977, she released *Two Days Away* from which came the hit singles *Pearl's a Singer* and *Sunshine After the Rain*. In 1978, she released *Shooting Star* and the following year came *Live and Learn*, which gave her the hit singles *Lilac Wine* and *Don't Cry Out Loud*.

(Middle). Formed in Oldham in 1966 by John Lees, Les Holroyd, Mel Pritchard and Stewart Wolstenholme, progressive rock group *Barclay James Harvest* are pictured here with some of the six tons of equipment, including amplifiers and mixing panel, they were taking with them on their European tour. Also travelling with the tour was a forty-piece orchestra under Robert Godfrey.

Originally signed to EMI/Parlophone, the group released their debut album *Barclay James Harvest* in June 1970 to critical acclaim though it was not commercially successful. It was a similar story with their next three albums: *Once Again, Barclay James Harvest* and *Other Stories and Baby James Harvest*. In 1974 the group moved to Polydor where their fortunes changed for the better. The debut album for Polydor, *Everyone is Everybody Else*, led to John Peel inviting them onto his BBC Radio 1 show. In December 1974, *Barclay James Harvest Live*, entered the UK album charts and reached number 40. It was followed in October 1975 by *Time Honoured Ghost* (reached number 32 in UK album charts) and in October 1976 by *Octoberon* (reached number 19 in UK album charts). The following April, they released an EP, *Live*, which made it to number 49 in the UK singles charts. Before the decade was out they released two more albums: *Gone to Earth* (reached number 30) and *Barclay James Harvest XII* (reached number 31). It was after *XII* that keyboards player Stewart Wolstenholme left. Wolstenholme's playing of the mellotron had featured heavily in the group's repertoire.

(Bottom). As the 1960s drew to a close, the Hollies were still turning out hits, including *Sorry Suzanne, He Ain't Heavy, He's My Brother* and the album *The Hollies Sing Dylan*. In December 1969, Graham Nash left and moved to the US, where he formed Crosby, Stills & Nash with Stephen Stills (ex-Buffalo Springfield) and Dave Crosby (ex-Byrds). Nash's place in the Hollies was taken by Terry Sylvester (ex-Swinging Blue Jeans), who also joined the group's song writing team. Two singles released during

1970, *I Can't Tell the Bottom from the Top* and *Gasoline Alley Bred*, reached numbers seven and fourteen respectively in the UK, whilst their album Confessions of the Mind reached number 30.

However, Alan Clarke was concerned over the direction the band was heading in. He left in 1971 and was replaced as lead vocalist by Swede Mikael Rickfors. In 1972, the single *Magic Touch Woman* became the first official Hollies release since 1963 to fail to chart in the UK. When Alan Clarke re-joined during 1973, home market sales began to pick up. *The Day That Curly Billy Shot Down Sam McGee* reached number 24 and the follow-up single *The Air That I Breathe* reached number two. The band also released three UK hit albums: *Hollies* (number 38), *Hollies Hits Live* (number four) and *20 Golden Greats* (number two).

(Right and Bottom). David Cassidy and fans at Belle Vue, March 1973. In 1972, he had UK hits with *Could It Be Forever*, *How Can I Be Sure* and *Rock Me Baby.*

Formed by Brian Ferry and Graham Simpson in late 1970, early 1971, Roxy Music were on the avant-garde end of glam rock. Some of this was due to the influence of Brian Eno, who, though not a musician in the accepted sense of the word, could operate a synthesizer and was a conceptual/electronics genius. The band released their first album, *Roxy Music*, in 1972, followed the same year by their first single *Virginia Plain*, which reached number four in the UK charts. Their second album, *For Your Pleasure*, was released in March 1973. Soon after Brian Eno left over differences with Brian Ferry and was replaced by the former Curved Air multi-instrumentalist Eddie Jobson. Another addition to the band was the former Merseybeats bass guitarist, John Gustafson, who played on three studio albums but did not always tour with the band. Roxy Music's next two albums, *Stranded* and *Country Life*, are acknowledged as being amongst the finest examples of British art rock of the 1970s. Their 1978 album, *Manifesto*, gave the band two UK top-ten singles hits. *Angel Eyes* reached number four and *Dance Away* reached number two. Roxy Music headlined two gigs at Belle Vue. The first was on 18 October 1974, the second was on 14 October 1976.

Cum on feel the noize. Jim Lea and Noddy Holder of Slade do their stuff at Belle Vue in 1974. Slade were at the height of their fame in the UK. The albums *Slayed* and *Slayed Alive* are considered by many to be the best of the glam rock era. In early 1973, their single *Cum on Feel the Noize* was the first since the Beatles Get Back in 1969 to go straight to number one in the UK charts on release. Their last UK number one single was *Merry Xmas Everyone*, released for Christmas 1973, though *Far, Far Away*, made it to number two in 1974. Their album *Old, New, Borrowed and Blue* reached number two in February 1974.

(Above). Rod Stewart performing with the Faces at Belle Vue on 24 November 1974.

Denis Law presents Rod Stewart with a gold disc marking sales worth £150,000 for his album *Sing it again Rod*.

Northern Soul disc jockey Russ Winstanley at Wigan Casino holds a copy of the remix single *Footsee*. Originally released in 1968 by the Canadian band The Chosen Few, this was the first ever commercially successful remix of a previously released track. Under the name Wigan's Chosen Few, it enjoyed an eleven-week run in the UK charts, reaching number nine. However, it was the 'B' side, *Seven Days Too Long* by Chuck Wood, that was deemed by many to be a true Northern Soul track. The sight of dancers from Wigan Casino on BBC TV's *Top of the Pops* dancing to Footsee was too much for some purists as it had the potential to push Northern Soul into the mainstream.

(Below). To a mixture of American soul, R&B, Motown and jazz, Northern Soul dance moves of the early 1970s were high energy and featured spins, high kicks, flips – even the splits for those athletic enough to do them.

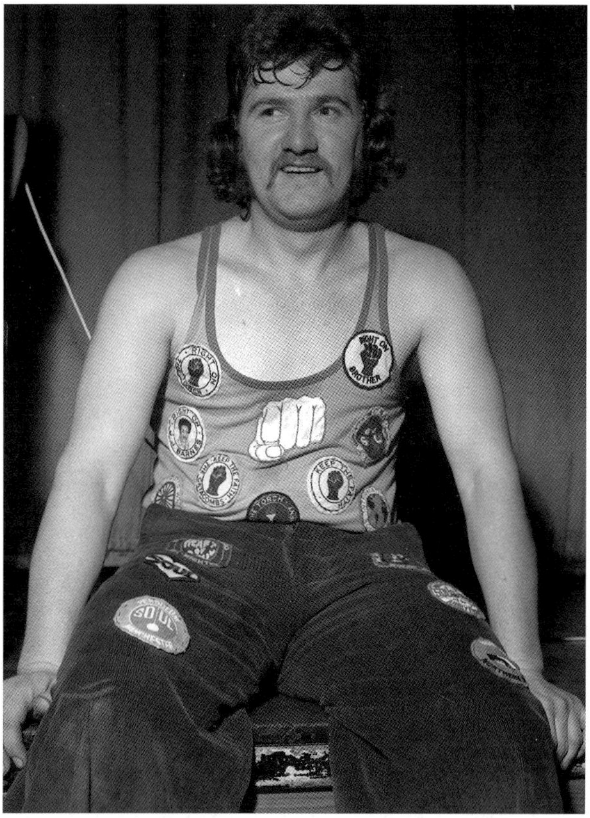

Scenes from Wigan Casino. Northern Soul dancers sported sew-on badges on their sports vests and Oxford trousers. The badges often represented soul club membership, though they also wore the clenched fist symbol of the Black Power movement in the United States.

Founded in Stockport, 10cc comprised former school friends Graham Gouldman, Lol Creme and Kevin Godley, and the former Mindbenders guitarist Eric Stewart. The four had worked together off and on since the late 1960s, recording at Strawberry Studios, Stockport. They formed 10cc in 1972, signing with Jonathan King's UK Records in July that same year. Three months later, their first single released on UK Records, *Donna*, went to number two in the charts. In June 1973, they had their first number one with *Rubber Bullets*, and three months after that *The Dean and I* made it to number ten. In February 1975, 10cc split with King over royalties and signed for Mercury Records. They are pictured here in April 1974, filming a take of their top-ten single *Life is a Minestrone* for BBC TV's *Top of the Pops*. This was made the lead single from their album *The Original Soundtrack* (released 1 January 1975), as the band thought their favourite track *I'm Not in Love* was, at six minutes, too long for the singles market. Anyway, the track was released in June 1975, giving 10cc their second UK number one and a US number two. In our image, left to right, we have: Lol Creme, Eric Stewart, Graham Gouldman and Kevin Godley.

(Opposite page). Phil Lynott of Thin Lizzy. Formed in Dublin, Ireland, in 1969, the group took their name from a character in the Dandy children's comic, Tin Lizzie. Their first single, released in July 1970, failed to chart as did their first album *Thin Lizzy*. The album includes a track, *Clifton Grange Hotel,* written about the Manchester hotel owned by Phil Lynott's mother. In May 1976, the group reached number six in the UK charts with *The Boys Are Back In Town*, about the group's visits to Manchester.

Singer, songwriter and record producer Barry White and his wife Glodean pictured in May 1975 during their UK tour with the Love Unlimited Orchestra. During the early 1970s, White had produced the girl group Love Unlimited, comprising Glodean, her sister Linda James and their cousin Diane Taylor. Their first single, *Walkin' in the Rain with the One I Love*, reached number fourteen in the UK and number six in the US Soul Singles Chart. It went on to sell more than one million copies. In 1975, they had their only US number one hit single with *I Belong to You*. The 40-piece Love Unlimited Orchestra was put together to back both Barry and Love Unlimited. They appeared at Belle Vue on 13 May 1975.

The Bay City Rollers hosted their own children's TV series, *Shang-a-lang*, produced by Granada TV in Manchester. The Rollers were allegedly the most screamed-at and screamed-about act of the decade, though David Cassidy probably ran them a close second. Between February 1974 and September 1976, they had nine top-ten hits of which *Bye Bye Baby* and *Give A Little Love* went to the top of the charts. They also had four top-ten albums, the first of which Rollin' went to number one and remained in the album charts for an impressive sixty-two weeks. Their second album, *Once Upon A Star*, also went to number one, remaining in the charts for thirty-seven weeks. The Rollers performed at Belle Vue on 12 September 1976.

The Stranglers in Manchester for their gig at the Electric Circus, 5 June 1977. As can be seen, base-guitarist JJ Burnel's right hand is heavily bandaged following a bit of a to-do the previous night at the Wigan Casino. *Sunday Mirror* journalist Colin Wills described Burnel's heavily bandaged hands as looking 'like they've recently been fed to an alligator'.

This image of fans at The Stranglers' Manchester Electric Circus gig on 5 June 1977 was taken by Brian Randle of the *Sunday Mirror*. The following week it was used to illustrate Colin Wills' front-page lead, PUNK ROCK JUBILEE SHOCKER. What's burning up the kid's? A disturbing report on the amazing new cult. PUNK-ROCK – the spitting, swearing, savage pop music of rebellious youth – is sweeping teenage Britain. Wills' report did not immediately focus on The Stranglers, but on the Sex Pistols and the fact that their single, *God Save The Queen*, was about to top the charts despite the BBC and some commercial stations refusing to play it and some retailers refusing to stock it. Wills reported that the record might yet become the fastest-seller in pop music history.

The Stranglers at Manchester during their tour. Released by United Artists, *Rattus Norvegicus* reached number four in the UK album charts and went platinum. Their second album *No More Heroes* reached number two and went gold. The single *No More Heroes* was a top-ten hit, reaching number eight. They also performed a gig at Belle Vue on 13 October 1977.

If everyone who claimed to have been at the Lesser Free Trade Hall on 4 June 1977 had been there, then the place would have been heaving. As it was, an estimated 35-40 people turned up to see the Sex Pistols. That said, those 35-40 people included two students from Bolton Institute of Technology, Pete Shelley and Howard De Voto, who went on to form the Buzzcocks. Also there was Tony Wilson who was involved with Granada TV's culture and music programme *So It Goes*. To Wilson, the Sex Pistols were a breath of fresh air and he did not hesitate in booking them for what was probably the first TV performance by a punk band. Wilson also went on to found Factory Records.

Also present were the following: Mark E Smith, who went on to form the punk band The Fall; Bernard Sumner and Peter Hook, who went on to form Joy Division; Martin Hannett, who became a co-founder of Factory Records and produced records for the likes of Joy Division, John Cooper Clarke and the Happy Mondays, and music journalist Paul Morley, who would also manage Manchester punk band the Drones. Then there was young Steven Morrissey. He would soon join local band The Nosebleeds, co-writing several songs including, *I Get Nervous* and *Peppermint Heaven*. He later joined Slaughter and The Dogs but severed his ties when a recording deal fell through. There followed a stint as a journalist with Record Mirror and, in May 1982, Morrissey and Johnny Marr co-founded The Smiths.

Souxsie and the Banshees supported The Clash on their first UK tour. They also appeared with the Buzzcocks, and the Penetration, at Belle Vue on 17 December 1977.

(Opposite page). The Clash at the Elizabethan ballroom, Belle Vue, during their 32-date *Get Out of Control* Tour of the UK, Sweden, Germany and Ireland. Left to right: drummer Nicky 'Topper' Headon, lead vocalist/rhythm guitarist Joe Strummer, bassist Paul Simonon and vocalist/lead guitarist Mick Jones.

They were also in Manchester on 29 October, when they appeared at the Apollo, supported by Souxsie and the Banshees. The Clash's set included: *London's Burning*, *Complete Control*, *Clash City Rockers*, *Hate and War*, *Police and Thieves*, and the ska rhythm (*White Man*) *In Hammersmith Palais*. They returned to Manchester on 15 November to play at Belle Vue, where their set included *Capital Radio*, *Janie Jones*, *What's My Name* and *Garageland*.

positive

EXIT

That's Entertainment

Former members of the cast of *Coronation Street* get together to celebrate the tenth anniversary of the show. Standing, left to right: Graham Haberfield, Arthur Lowe, Brian Rawlinson, Ernst Waldner, Nigel Humphreys, Jack Smethurst, Gordon Rollings and Reg Marsh. Seated, left to right: Susan Jameson, Renny Lister, Christine Hargreaves, Doris Hare, Frank Pemberton and Noel Dyson. Seated, Kenneth Cope.

William Roache, alias Corrie's Ken Barlow, but not as you might expect. He is seen here in November 1970, wearing a mini dress for his part as King Pentheus in John Bowen's play *The Disorderly Women*.

In February 1974, Violet Carson asked to be written out of Corrie due to ill health and her character Ena Sharples left to live in St Annes. Violet returned to the Street in October 1975.

In 1974, Susi Hush replaced Eric Prytherch as Corrie's producer. It was Susi Hush's idea to give Corrie a continental edge by filming two episodes in Majorca. Scriptwriter Adele Rose's storyline being that Bet Turpin wins a Spot-the-Ball competition and invites seven of the ladies on a week's holiday. The cast stayed in a hotel full of real-life holidaymakers and much of the filming was done in and around the hotel and its pool.

Smile please. Among the guests at Gail Potter and Brian Tilsley's wedding were: Stan Ogden (Bernard Youens), Hilda Ogden (Jean Alexander), Ena Sharples (Violet Carson), Albert Tatlock (Jack Haworth), Dierdre Barlow (Anne Kirkbride), Ken Barlow (William Roache), Audrey Potter (Sue Nicholls), Jack Duckworth (Bill Tarmey) and Vera Duckworth (Elizabeth Dawn).

Actresses Clare Sutcliffe (left) and Anne Kirkbride on location in the Manchester area on 25 October 1971, filming *Another Sunday and Sweet F.A.* - a one-off drama by Jack Rosenthal for Granada TV's Sunday Night Theatre. Clare and Anne played footballers' girlfriends. Anne's performance led to her being offered the part of Deirdre Barlow in Corrie. Anne got her acting break whilst working as a student assistant stage manager at Oldham Rep when director Carl Paulson offered her full-time acting at £18 a week.

One of Granada TV's hits of 1970 was the comedy series *The Lovers*, starring Paula Wilcox (20) as Beryl Battersby and Richard Beckinsale (23) as Geoffrey Scrimshaw. Written by Jack Rosenthal, the show ran for two series totalling thirteen episodes. Beryl referred to Geoffrey as 'Geoffrey bubbles bonbon' and sex as 'percy filth'.

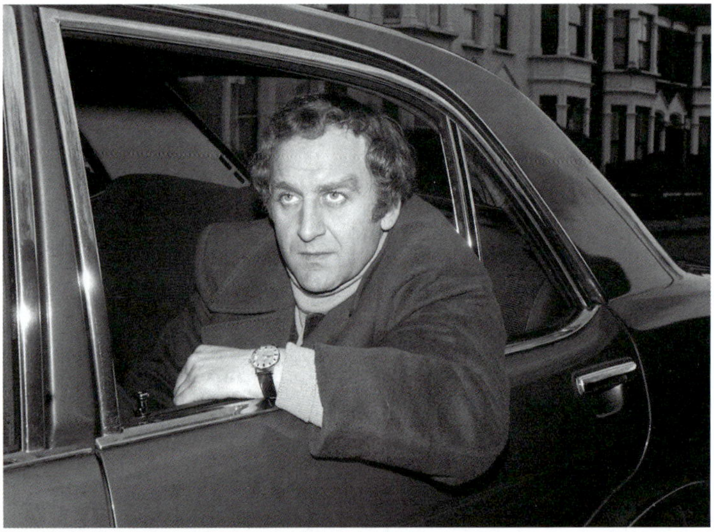

Born in Longsight and growing up in Gorton and Burnage, John Thaw was accepted for the Royal Academy of Dramatic Arts (RADA) in 1958. Within a couple of years of leaving RADA, he secured his first starring role, playing Sergeant John Mann in the ABC Weekend TV series *Redcap*. Appearances in other TV series such as *Inheritance and Budgie* followed. Our image was taken in November 1974, during filming for a new cop series from Thames Television called *The Sweeney*. Thaw, cast as detective inspector Jack Regan and Dennis Waterman as detective sergeant George Carter, are members of the Met's no-nonsense Flying Squad; tackling armed robbery and violent crime in seventies London. The Sweeney was an instant hit, running for four series and proving popular enough for two spin-off feature films to be made. Thaw is pictured here leaning out of a Ford Consul Granada MKI GT, one of the great cars of the 1970s.

Vanessa Redgrave rehearsing Henrik Ibsen's *The Lady from The Sea*, at the Royal Exchange Theatre, October 1978.

(Above). Glam-rocker Marc Bolan of T Rex in July 1975 during rehearsals for Granada TV's *Rock on with 45*. In 1977, Granada broadcast the six-part series *Marc*, which was hosted by Bolan and went out live.

(Above right). Bury singer-songwriter Peter Skellern had just completed a series of programmes for BBC television featuring northern brass bands. In 1972, his debut single, *You're A Lady*, reached number three in the UK charts, followed in 1975 by *Hold On to Love*, which reached number fourteen. In 1973, he sang the theme song for the TV series *Billy Liar*.

(Right). Strawberry Studios, Stockport, is world famous and for many of us it will always be associated with the song-writing, recording and production talent that was 10cc. Laying down a vinyl or two in June 1972 are Lancashire County Cricket Club. David Lloyd is on the right of the picture.

Facebook Memories

Winefride Street – Nice picture of Marc Bolan. Loved Ride a White Swan, one of his many great records. Sad when he died he was only young, what a waste of good talent.

Catherine Ucer – Loved this man. Went to see him at The Free Trade Hall Manchester.

The Manchester cast for the musical *Hair* seen here during rehearsals at the Palace Theatre in February 1970. At the top of the pile is a young Paul Barber, who was making his stage debut. His first major role came in 1974, when he played Sam *'Lucky'* Ubootu in the ITV Playhouse drama Lucky, made by Granada TV. He is best known for his role as Denzil in *Only Fools and Horses*. The soundtrack and plot lines of the stage (1968) and film (1979) versions of *Hair* differ. Four original songs were omitted altogether from the movie, though a new one, *Somebody to Love*, was added. Five further original songs were recorded but cut during the movie's editing.

There were fishnet tights, sequins – and goose pimples – in chilly Oxford Street on 18 December 1970. *Manchester Evening News* photographer Eric Graham snapped the Television Toppers demonstrating their high-kicking routine outside the Palace Theatre. The Toppers were opening that night's *Black and White Minstrel Show*, the stage version of what was, in the Seventies, one of the most popular light entertainment programmes on television. The show was scheduled to run at the Palace until 20 March 1971. For minstrel soloist Peter Pennington – who came from Eccles - it was his second show back home since joining the company in 1966. Other locals in the show were minstrel Chris Connah from Droylsden and Topper Liz Lax from Oldham.

The Palace Theatre, November 1977.

Palace Theatre administrator Bob Scott surveys the work being done to rip out the old stage. The £3million restoration project aimed at making it one of the biggest and best venues in Europe. A public appeal raised £1.5million, the remainder coming from the Arts Council, business, and local authorities. The work took three years to complete, the Palace reopening with a production of *Jesus Christ Superstar* by Andrew Lloyd Webber and Tim Rice.

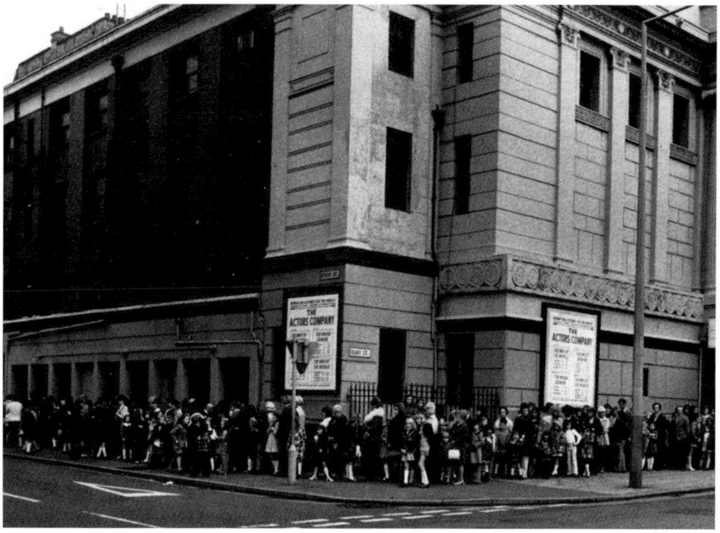

This queue at the Opera House, Manchester, in November 1973 wasn't to see a performance – these kids were hopefuls auditioning for the parts as Diddymen in an upcoming Ken Dodd show. Only a fraction of the queue is shown here as it carried on along Quay Street. At the time, the Opera House Actors Company had two productions on – Chekov's *The Wood Demon* and William Congreve's *The Way of the World*.

The 1978 Christmas pantomime at the Opera House, Manchester, was *Dick Whittington*. It starred Basil Brush, Ayshea (as Dick Whittington) and the special guest star was comedian Frank Carson (wearing glasses). Also appearing were Radio Piccadilly's Phil Wood and Bert Weedon (with guitar). Frank Carson was a regular performer on Granada TV's *The Comedians* along with Charlie Williams, Jim Bowen and Mike Reid.

Opening night at Manchester's new £1million theatre – the Royal Exchange. September 1976.

Tom Courtenay and Judi Bowker rehearsing a scene from Richard Sheridan's comedy *The Rivals* at the Royal Exchange Theatre, 6 September 1976.

Salford-born actor Albert Finney pictured in February 1977, during rehearsals for *Uncle Vanya* at the Royal Exchange.

What a choice for cinemagoers. The Gaumont is showing the action-packed drama *The Professionals*, starring Burt Lancaster, Lee Marvin, Jack Palance, Claudia Cardinale and Robert Ryan. Originally released in 1966, *The Professionals*, had three nominations for the 1967 Academy Awards and won the 1967 *Motion Picture Magazine* Laurel Awards for Best Action Drama and Best Action Performance. Though *The Professionals* had its UK premier in London in June 1967, the movie was re-released in some countries during 1972. The Oxford on the other hand is screening the 23rd movie in the highly successful Carry On franchise, *Carry on Abroad*.

Released in December 1972, *Carry on Abroad* featured the regular cast apart from Jim Dale and Terry Scott. It was Charles Hawtrey's last appearance in a Carry On and June Whitfield's first since *Carry on Nurse* in 1959. The plot centres around a package holiday tour to Spain, where, on arrival, the guests find they are holidaying amid a building site. Producer Peter Rogers was never one to throw money around so filming was done at Pinewood Studios; the studio car park being covered with sand. Comedian Jimmy Logan appeared in the movie and in one scene he falls into wet cement. The cement was in fact porridge died grey. In the opening credits, Sun Tao Lo Tion is credited as Technical Adviser, in other words Suntan Lotion. When *Carry on Abroad* premiered on TV, it attracted 18million viewers.

By the late 1960s – early 70s, cinema seat prices were rising faster than inflation, though at the same time attendances were falling. In 1946, UK cinemas attracted 1,635million customers. By 1960, attendances had fallen to around 500million and were down to 200million in 1970. The industry was not going down without a fight and though many super cinemas like the Gaumont were closed, others were converted into two, three or even four-screen venues.

Manchester Odeon's Wurlitzer organ on its way to the Lancastrian Theatre Organ Trust following its donation by the Rank Organisation. Following restoration, the trust donated it to Manchester Corporation who installed it in the Free Trade Hall in 1977.

(Right). Dating back to 1914, the Market Street Picture House underwent several incarnations prior to becoming the Cinephone Cinema in 1955. The Cinephone specialised in showing output from European studios – usually sub-titled French or Italian films and in the 1960s it became 'infamous' for screening Continental erotic movies. Indeed, the last films screened here were *Where Are You Going All Naked* and *The Queer, The Erotic*. The only thing 'foreign' in our image which is thought to date from the summer of 1973, is the Cinephone's showing today signs AUJOURD'HUI, OGGI and HEUTE. On offer to cinema fans are *The Bofors Gun* and *Strictly For The Birds*, both of which featured actors from the Manchester area. In *The Bofors Gun*, Longsight-born actor John Thaw played Gunner Featherstone and Manchester-born actor David Warner played Lance Bombardier Terry 'Lance Bar' Evans. Another actor with soon-to-be Manchester connections was Geoffrey Hughes who played Private Samuel. Hughes is better known to Corrie fans as binman Eddie Yates. *Strictly For The Birds* featured Salford-born actress Christine Hargreaves, an original cast member of Corrie in which she played Christine Hardman. The cinema closed on 14 January 1974 and was demolished to make way for the Arndale Centre.

These ladies from Manila worked at a mill in Rochdale and are pictured here giving a display Pilipino dancing. July 1972.

Carnival time at Alexandra Park, 1978.

Feeding time for the elephants, 25 August 1970. Following Belle Vue zoo's closure, all the animals except one had found new homes. *Ellie May* the elephant had acquired a reputation for being difficult and zoos were reluctant to take her. Despite having left, former zoo superintendent Peter Grayson continued to visit *Ellie May* and feed her. Eventually, Rotterdam Zoo agreed to take her but she refused to enter the packing crate becoming very distressed. Overnight she developed pneumonia and heart failure. Grayson consulted David Taylor, the first veterinary surgeon in the world to specialise in zoo and wildlife medicine. It was clear to Taylor that *Ellie May* would not recover and the decision was taken to put her down.

Over in the Belle Vue children's zoo, gerbils Gerry and Joan have moved into a new home – an old suede boot that belonged to their keeper. October 1972.

Hercules takes a last dip before being transferred to Cleethorpes Zoo. When Cleethorpes closed, he was moved to Dudley Zoo where he eventually died of peritonitis.

Belle Vue Zoo superintendent Peter Grayson with *Blanco* the lion who he had raised from a cub when his mother deserted him. Because of his affinity with humans – he would often go on walks with Grayson - *Blanco* could not be returned to the main lion enclosure.

Topaz the chimp with a group of Cheshire schoolchildren who had collected 50tons of waste paper to be used as shredabeds for the animals. November 1976.

The end of an era. Taken on 20 August 1977, the card this chimp is holding tells it all. The zoo was losing an estimated £100,000 a year and, rather than invest, its owners decided to pull the plug. The keepers were told the news just one hour before it was announced on the BBC. Most of the animals were found new homes at other zoos, though some of the snakes and reptiles even went home with their former keepers.

Jacko the clown squirts water from his hat as he walks around the edge of the circus ring. December 1978.